AJ's FOOD ROOTS

Dedication

For Barbara.
You are my wife, my soul mate and my support.
You have stood by me and piece by piece made me a better man.
You have given me two beautiful kids and made my life complete.
With all my love.

Published by
Landmark Books Pte Ltd
5001 Beach Road,
02-73/74
Singapore 199588

Landmark Books is an imprint of Landmark Books Pte Ltd

ISBN 978-981-4189-58-3

Printed in Singapore

Andrew Johnson
AJ's FOOD ROOTS
SOUTHEAST ASIAN AND SRI LANKAN FLAVOURS

·LANDMΛRK·BOOKS·

CONTENTS

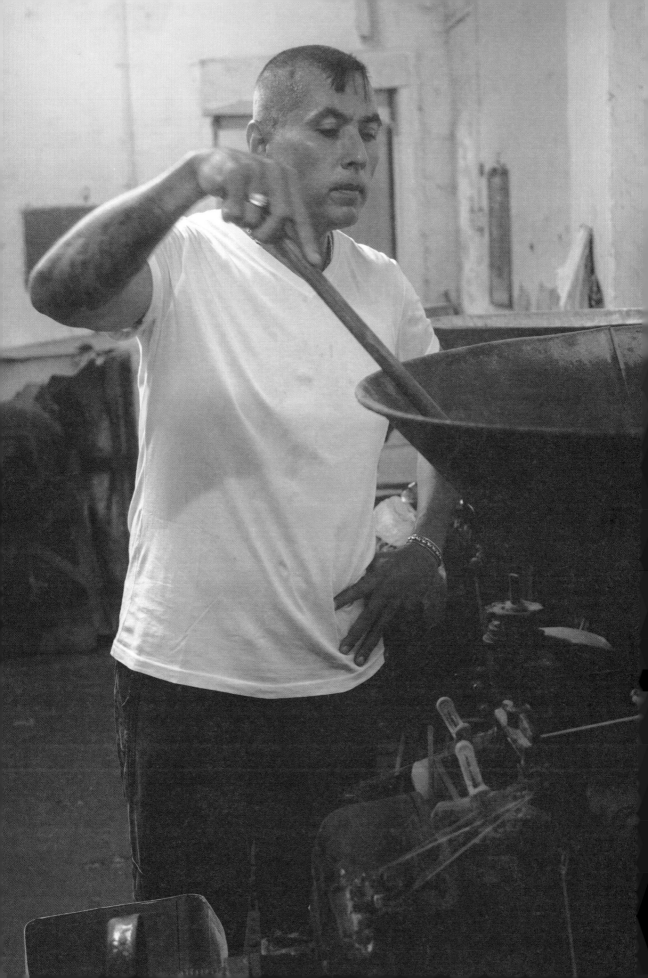

MY STORY SO FAR

I MUST HAVE BEEN around 4 years old enjoying a curry, sitting at the dinner table with mum and dad, when my surprised, puzzled and multi-expressioned face drew their attention. Mum laughed and said, "Andy's got the bomb!"

A cardamom, a small seedpod, triangular in cross-section and spindle-shaped, with a thin, papery outer shell and small black seeds nested within. Its strong, unique taste that is intensely aromatic was my first introduction to a dry spice.

Growing up, it was not uncommon for me to be sent into the garden to get some karuvepillai (curry leaf), daun limau purut (kaffir lime leaf), serai (lemongrass), daun kaduk (betel leaf), lengkuas (blue ginger or galangal), kunyit (turmeric root), or daun pandan (pandanus leaf). These herbs and roots are common ingredients in the cuisine of Southeast Asia, and as I grew older, I was exposed to their medicinal values as well.

The 1980s were not yet the high tech, touch screen era (yes I am from the generation where we wound our cassette tapes with 2B pencils). Satisfying curiosity and finding amusement as a kid for me was often in the kitchen storeroom. I recall dabbling with different spices when no one was watching – some looked like stars (star anise), some like tree bark (cinnamon), some like little flowers (cloves), tiny black ball bearings (mustard seeds), and what I thought were rice grains (fennel seeds). I used to think, could I plant a star tree? Would it be covered in tiny stars? If you're wondering if I tried it, well, yes I did.

My first experience with the medicinal properties of spices came about when I was around 9 years old. One morning, after too many sticks of sweets, I woke up with the mother of all toothaches. I can remember literally wanting to pound my head into the wall. Mum gave me a Panadol, but to no avail. Sitting in the kitchen, I was very dramatic. My grandma quietly went into the storeroom and took out the *batu tumbuk* (motar and pestle) and began pounding. When she was done, she walked over to me and said, "Open your mouth." She proceeded to rub my gums with something powdery. In a matter of seconds, the pain subsided as my gums felt numb. This was the day I learnt about the magic properties of the little black flower bud known as the clove.

Soon, I noticed spices, herbs and roots were in so many foods in all the cultures of Southeast Asia. Basics like rice was cooked with pandan leaf (*pandanus*), cloves, star anise, cardamoms, cinnamon, and kunyit (turmeric root). Barley was cooked with a few slices of ginger root, serai (lemongrass) or mint leaves. Lime juice – tradionally made with limau kasturi (calamansi/calamondin) or key lime (limau nipis) – had asam boi (fermented prunes), mint, kaffir lime rind and even peppercorns added to them. It began to amaze me, and I soon found that not only diverse flavors were attained when they were used in cooking, but these little gems were also part of natural remedies passed down from generation to generation.

In my teens, a different form of spice was of more of an interest, the kind that fires you up one day, and makes you a love-sick puppy the next. But that's a story for another day. By 14, I was already working part-time in a hotel as a kitchen hand and waitering as well. I was still in school but, after classes, all I could think about was the world of food and beverage. Sauces and spices, filleting and deboning. Picking up new skills (yes I am skilled with a cleaver), and really having a good time in the kitchen.

Fishing, too, was a big part of my life. Every chance I got I was out at sea with my dad, or casting a net by the shoreline, gathering clams, setting up fishing rigs, and laying traps for crabs.

I got into a lot of trouble in school when I was 16. I got suspended and was only allowed to commence school the following year for my final year. Admitedly, I had become a rebellious teen. My dad spoke to the family priest who knew a local fisherman. And this is how I met Uncle Goh.

I needed to find myself. I needed to understand. I needed, in my own way, my freedom. It was at this time that I learnt that with this need came great responsibility. I would be up by 4.30 am, bicycle down to the market where I met Uncle Goh for a cup of tea and a bun or some nasi lemak. At 5 am, he would have me swim half a mile out to sea in the pitch darkness, guided only by the echo of waves softly thumping the side of a wooden sampan. Climbing onto the boat, I was greeted by the wind (and it was cold), the I would proceed to haul in the anchor and row to the shore. Then we would load up the nets and proceed to the fishing spots which were chosen after Uncle Goh had read the conditions of the water, tides, wind direction and – if you will believe me – the sounds from the seabed.

By midday, we would head back to shore and the day's catch – fish, crabs, prawns and squid – would then be taken to the market where yours truly was the fish monger talking to the aunties, bargaining, filleting fish, recommending seafood for curries, fried or steamed recipes. At the end of the day, Uncle Goh would ask me to take some fish home for mum and dad. At first I did but, one day, Uncle Goh gave me 5 ringgit and well, I must admit, from that day on, I didn't bring much fish home, because I was getting paid. It did not dawn upon me until about a month later, with calluses and blisters on my fingers, stings from jellyfish, and jabs from standing on sea urchins, that I asked myself, "Is what I am doing with my life worth 5 ringgit?" It was an honest living, and I first understood both the meaning of responsibility and the value of money at that point.

I continued till the year end, and later, I obtained my boat licence and took on a job with a sailing company where fishing, diving and sailing took me from Penang up to the Andaman Islands. About a year and a half later, Uncle Goh passed away. Remembering the last time I saw him, I am happy we shared this time together, and he made a change in my life.

Once school ended, I asked my dad to send me to culinary school. It was all I wanted to do. Hotel school was great, and everything was well in my perfect little world. I was working, and studying what I loved most. Then in a flash, my life took a drastic turn. Going home, I was hit by a car. Broken toes, shin, knee and thigh, cracked ribs and collarbone. Lying on the ground, there was this eerie silence, and I thought: Well, I am dead.

Rushed to the emergency room. Lying on the cold steel table (felt like a piece of meat). Everyone buzzing around me. By 2 am, my father and mother walked into the ward to find me sitting up, all plastered up but throwing cotton balls at other patients saying, "wheeeeeee". I was probably high on morphine.

As time passed in hospital, I sank into a self pity. "Why aren't more people visiting me? Am I that bad a person? What do I do now? The doctor said I won't be able to walk for another six months and, if I did, I would hobble."

When I was finally discharged and all the plaster was removed, therapy followed. Modern heat treatment (where they immerse your leg in hot wax) did not seem to work. Discomfort and irritability set in. One of the nurses, seeing my frustration, proceeded to tell me about traditional cures. A few days later, I went to see a traditional Malay doctor. His treatment began with heated clove oil and star anise for the aches and bone pain. He wrapped my leg in pounded ginger to reduce the swelling. He made me drink the boiled root of tongkat ali (*Eurycoma longifolia*) to flush the kidneys and liver of impurities. (Yes, it's also an aphrodisiac.) So, despite the doctor saying that I would not walk for six months, I strolled into his office two months later and gave him back his crutches.

I do not know if it was a sign from God for me to slow down but, when I talked to my mum about it, we agreed that God works in mysterious ways, and when you are on the wrong path in life, he steers you back. So, at the age of 20, I moved to Singapore where I started a new career running the front desk at the newly restored Raffles Hotel.

Cooking at the time was more for parties and to feed myself. My time off from work was again with fishing adventures, and from the mid-1990s, I started to travel across Southeast Asia, often sitting by road-side stalls in Thailand, Indonesia, Vietnam and even Nepal eating the real food of thre region. Then, one day, I ended up on the spice streets of Kochi, Kerala, on the Malabar coast of India. It was here, that I was able to combine the knowledge of spices from home, with that of Southeast Asia and Sri Lanka with a greater in-depth understanding.

I must say the people of Sri Lanka and Kerala are beautiful (especially since my mother is of Sri Lankan-Dutch descent). The spice market of Kochi was a place of education. Every day, I would hear these words: "Spices are the blessing from mother earth."

One vendor explained, "Herbs are the leaves of soft green plants, while spices come from the roots, bark, and seeds. Like corinader, you use both leaves and seeds, and wild fennel where you can use the flowers for rice and the dried seeds for meats" I learnt of teas made from spices and later drank my first brew of cardamom spice tea in Nepal.

I was amazed by the deep history that spices have and their true origins. It gave me flashbacks of my "star tree", broken bones and that toothache when I was a child. Spice mills, lime stone pestles, *batu giling* (metate) – all these instruments ground the same spices in different ways for different kinds of cooking methods. Every Asian country has its own style, their own way of using herbs and spices. Galangal (blue ginger, lengkuas) as an essential ingredient in Thai cuisine. It is daun salam (Indonesian laurel) that gives Indonesian cuisine its distinct aroma. So, serai (lemongrass) in Malaysian cuisine, mint in Vietnamese food, cinnamon in Keralan dishes, asafoetida (giant fennel) in Nepalese fare, sesame oil that flavours Chinese cooking, and tumeric in Indian curries. I began to write new recipes, and make my own curry powders and spice mixes.

Wanting to take my knowledge to a new level, I left the corporate world and opened Spice Tree, a little curry puff shop in the heart of Geylang. Here, I was greeted by customers with a look of surprise, "Ang moh (European) selling curry puffs?" I ground my own spice mix as I wanted my puffs to be different. Barely two months after opening in 2004, *The Straits Times* in a blind tasting with a line up of food celebrities like Violet Oon and KF Seetoh voted me as the maker of the best curry puffs in Singapore, giving me the title "Puff Daddy". I was the first to make the spectaular durian-filled puffs which took the market by storm, which attracted copycats. I also made mango custard and apple puffs as I felt the kids need something special too. To this day, my fans want my sardine puffs and hae bee hiam puffs even though I have moved on to distributing the wines of Marco Bacci, one of the best winemakers in Italy.

Still, spices and herbs opened a new path in life for me. An interest became a passion that I want to share. I want people to relate to these recipes as I do. I want people to feel what these recipes are about, where they came from and how they have touched the lives of people who have been on this journey with me, from this book to the next.

A FEW TRICKS

HOW TO MAKE SPICE POWDERS
Spice powders are key marinades. Although there are many types available commercially, making your own spice mix is always best.

Spice powder for meat and seafood
150 g (5 oz) coriander seeds
80 g (3 oz) dried chillies
15 g (0.5 oz) star anise
1 teaspoon cloves
1 teaspoon aniseed
10 g (0.35 oz) cinnamon
10 g (0.35 oz) peppercorns
15 g (0.5 oz) fenugreek (halba)
10 g (0.35 oz) grated nutmeg
15 g (0.5 oz) fennel (jintan manis)
15 g (0.5 oz) cumin (jintan putih)
25 g (0.88 oz) turmeric

Dry fry in a wok till aromatic. Leave to cool, then grind in spice grinder. Store in an air-tight jar or bottle.

European Spice Powder
5 g (0.15 oz) cinnamon
5 g (0.15 oz) grated nutmeg
10 g (0.35 oz) dried basil
10 g (0.35 oz) dried parsley
10 g (0.35 oz) dill
10 g (0.35 oz) fennel
10 g (0.35 oz) sea salt

In addition, you may wish to add the following:
10 g (0.35 oz) onion powder
5 g (0.15 oz) ginger powder
10 g (0.35 oz) paprika
10 g (0.35 oz) cumin

Most of these spices are available in dry form. Mix and dry in microwave for 2-3 minutes on high.

Chinese Five-spice Powder
1 tablespoon ground Szechuan pepper (or black peppercorns)
4 star anise
1 tablespoon fennel
½ teaspoon cloves
2 sticks (5 cm, 2 in) cinnamon
½ teaspoon sea salt
½ teaspoon white pepper

Combine all ingredients and grind in spice mill.

Mixed spices for fish
5 tablespoons coriander seeds
2 tablespoons cumin seeds
6 teaspoons fennel seeds
4 teaspoons fenugreek seeds
2 teaspoons ground turmeric
1 teaspoon ginger powder
6 dried chillies
12 white peppercorns

Dry fry all these ingredients in a pan, allow to cool then grind in a spice blender.

HOW TO PREPARE PRAWNS

Trimming prawn heads
With prawn heads being a delicacy in Asia, effort is made in cleaning and preparing them. Cut away the sharp points on the heads of the prawns. Remove the sand sack which is from the mouth to 1 cm (0.4 in) behind the eyes. Also remove the mud sack which is on the upper lobe and connects to the vein on the back. Do this by cutting from the back of the eyes down to the mouth. Larger prawn species tend to have more debris in the head and down the spine.

Deveining without cutting
There is a vein-like digestive tract that runs along the upper back of the prawn. Using the prawns natural curve, press the head towards the tail, creating an inverted U shape. Push a toothpick in between the segments on top of the prawn to dislodge the vein. Place your thumb against the toothpick gently and lift upwards and the entire vein will come out.

Removing the head
Hold the body of the prawn in one hand and use the thumb and forefinger of the other hand to twist the head off.

Butterflying Method 1
Remove the head and cut through the shell on top of the prawn from the head to the tail with a pair of kitchen scissors. Remove the vein.

Butterflying Method 2
Remove the head. Place the prawn on a flat cutting board, resting your palm on the prawn. Slowly, with a sharp knife in a horizontal position, cut the shell from the head to the tail, slicing through to the meat but not completely cutting the prawn into two. Remove the vein.

Removing the shell
Remove the head. Turn the prawn over and pull the shell open along the length of the belly, working from the head downwards, prising it open with your thumb and forefinger so that you can pull the flesh free. Leave the tail on or pull it off depending on your preference.

HOW TO PREPARE CRABS

To prepare crabs, lift off the flap on the underside of the crab, remove the carapace (top shell) and discard the spongy gills under the shell. Rinse and cut each crab into quarters. Leave the pincers on the upper left and right quarters. The top shell of the sea crab is often just placed as a decorative ornament on the dishes. Most of the time, I boil these separately in a pot with a teaspoon of salt, only to be placed on the presented dish.

For rock crabs, remove the top shell and the flap under the crab. Also detach the claw, thereafter cut the crab into quarters. Using the back of a spoon, crack the claws to ensure that the juices of the dish can seep into the claws. Cracking the claws before serving the dish also makes eating it a lot easier.

STEAMING FISH

Steaming methods vary. You can use a steamer where the water is placed in the lower section and the fish, put in a heat-proof dish, is placed in the upper section for steaming. More common in Asia is the use of the wok where approximately 3 cups of water is brought to a light simmer, thereafter a trivet is placed just above the waterline enabling you to place the fish in a dish for steaming. Steaming is always done with a lid on to keep the steam within the wok or steamer. Strips of lemon rind, kaffir lime leaf, nutmeg, tea, and even lavender can be put in the water while the fish is steaming. Aroma therapy in the kitchen!

Determining the appropriate steaming time, according to the size of the fish, is crucial. I cook fish for 8 minutes per 2½ cm (1 in) of thickness. Hold the fish with its belly in your palm and putting your thumb and index finger around the fish will give you the approximate thickness. Timing starts when you put the fish into the steamer. This is done after the water is brought to a boil in the wok or steamer.

Always bear in mind that fish will continue to cook for a further 1-2 minutes after the heat is turned off. Lifting the lid at the 8 minute mark (irrespective of the thickness of the fish), and bathing the fish with the stock collected in the dish is what I always do.

The eyes of the fish turning white is one indication that the fish is cooked. That a skewer can easily slide through the meat to the bone is a second indication. If you have to use force to pierce the meat to reach the bone, then the fish is not yet cooked.

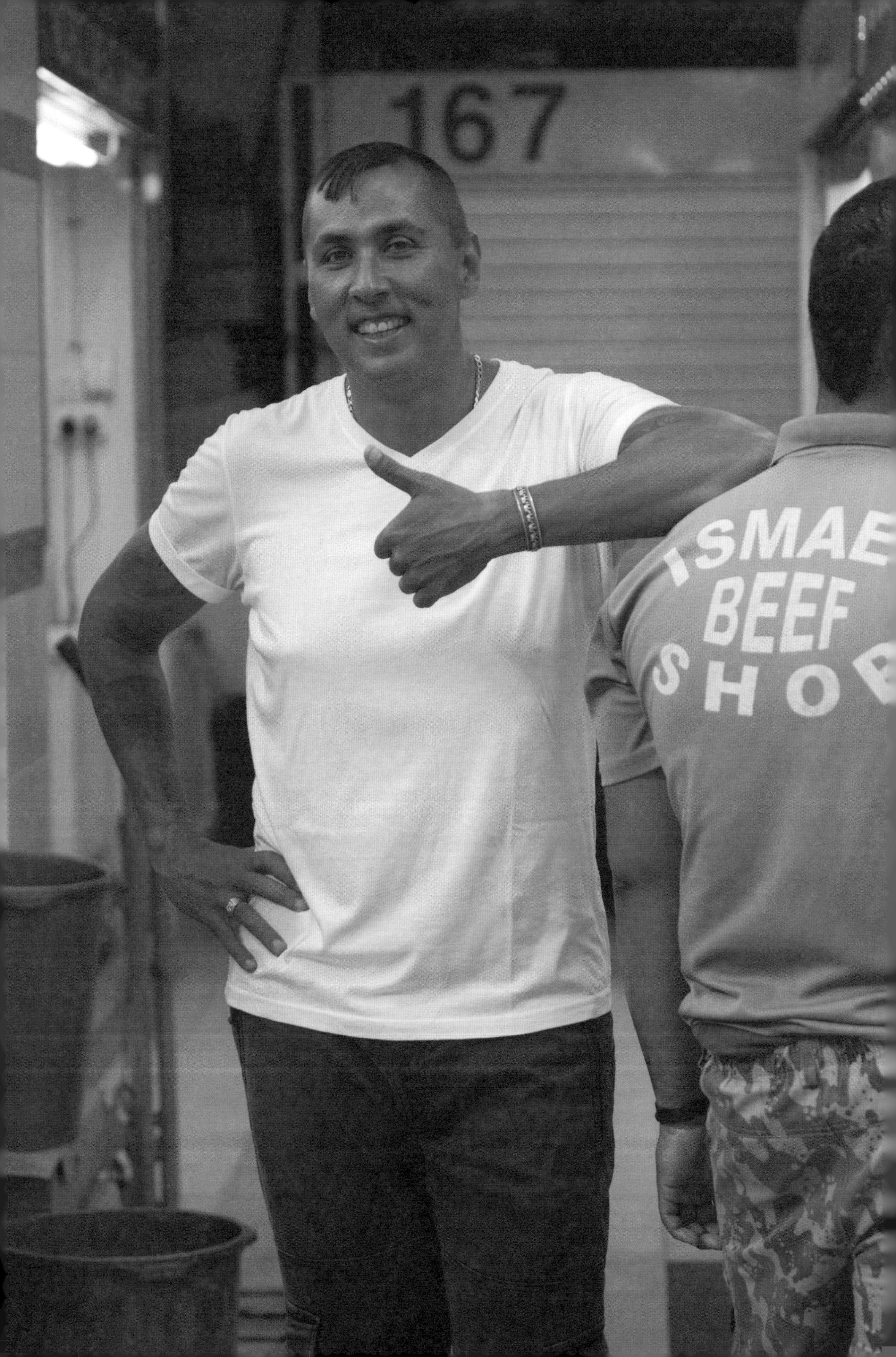
167
ISMAE
BEEF
SHOP

BEEF

GRANDMA'S SEMOR

The key ingredient in this recipe is the lime pickle. It is easy to make, and is used in a number of my unique recipes (see pages 32, 48). The pickled limes need about two weeks to ferment and be adequately pickeled for use, so make a batch of pickle ahead of time for this and other dishes.

¾ kg (1.65 lbs) beef, topside, shank or cross cut
1½ teaspoons palm sugar (gula Melaka)
4 tablespoons olive oil

Gravy ingredients
15 shallots or 2 large red onions, chopped
6 cloves garlic, chopped coarsely
5 cm (2 in) ginger, chopped
1 root end lemongrass (serai), bruised
2 sprigs curry leaves
5 cloves
4 cardamoms
¾ of a pickled calamansi lime (limau kesturi)
4 tablespoons meat curry powder
1 tablespoon chilli powder or paste
1 cup coconut milk
5 cm (2 in) cinnamon stick
Salt and sugar to taste

Mixed together
as an accompaniment to Semor
6 pickled calamansi limes (limau kesturi), seeds removed and limes chopped up finely
6 shallots, finely diced
1 red chilli, finely diced
1 teaspoon palm sugar (gula Melaka)
4 teaspoons vinegar from pickled lime

To make lime pickle
Wash and dry 25 calamansi limes (limau kesturi). Make a cross cut three-quarters through each lime.

Rub and pack the cut limes with 450 g (1 lb) salt and place them neatly with all the salt in a tray. Sun dry for 4-5 days, turning the limes in the salt daily, till they turn brownish and wrinkled.

Put the salted limes into a bottle or jar and fill with white vinegar. Refrigerate and rotate bottle every 2 days over a 2-week period.

The limes are ready to be used when they become soft and brown.

To make Semor
Put the beef into a deep saucepan followed by all the gravy ingredients. Add enough water to cover the beef. Give the ingredients a good stir to mix them up.

Bring to the boil, then lower heat to medium/low to simmer until the meat is cooked. Use a skewer to test the meat; the skewer should come out clean.

Take out the meat from the saucepan, leaving the gravy. Set the meat aside.

Heat 4 tablespoons of olive oil in a saucepan and fry the meat nicely on all sides. Slice the meat and return it and the oil used to fry the meat into the gravy. Add the 1½ teaspoons of palm sugar. Taste and adjust seasoning to your preferred taste.

Stir to ensure that all the meat is coated, thereafter simmer for a further 10-15 minutes on low heat to the point where you see the gravy is thick and the meat has soaked up most of the gravy.

MUM'S BEEF BONE CURRY

I must have been 6 years old when I first watched my mum make this dish, and in my innocence asked, "Mummy why are you cooking bones? Don't we have any chicken?"

1 kg (2.2 lbs) meaty beef bones
  (chuck or flank short ribs,
  bone in, also called country-
  style ribs)
½ cup coconut cream
3 slices dried 'tamarind'
  (assam gelugor, assam keping)
Palm sugar (gula Melaka)
  or brown sugar to taste
Salt to taste

Blended together
10 dried chillies, pre-soaked in
  hot water for about 5 minutes
4 fresh red chillies
4 cloves garlic
2 large red onions
5 cm (2 in) young ginger
1¼ cm (½ in) shrimp paste
  (belacan) cut widthwise from
  a 10 x 5 x 5 cm (5 x 2 x 2 in)
  block, toasted
4 candlenuts (buah keras)
2 root-ends lemongrass (serai)
1¼ cm (½ in) turmeric
  or ½ tsp turmeric powder
2½ cm (1 in) galangal (lengkuas)

Pour the coconut cream into a pan and cook on very low heat until oil separates from the cream.

Add the blended ingredients and fry till until aromatic and infused.

Now put in the beef bones and mix it well.

Put the prepared beef bones and blended spice mix into a pressure cooker. Pour in enough hot water to just cover the bones and pressure cook until soft, about 10-15 minutes.

The gravy should be nice and thick. Now add in the 'tamarind' slices and some palm sugar and salt to taste. Cook for a further 10 minutes in the pressure cooker under pressure until the meat is almost falling off the bone.

AJ's Notes: Should a pressure cooker not be available to you, you can use the same method in your regular pot still using hot water to cover the bones but cooking on a slow fire for 25-30 minutes. This is called the slow boil method. This method requires more observation and the occasional stir to ensure the ingredients do not stick to the bottom of the pan.

After 20 minutes, add in the 'tamarind' slices, salt and palm sugar to taste, thereafter continue to simmer for an additional 10-15 minutes. Ensure the texture is nice and thick, and the meat should be tender and falling off the bone.

My personal preference is to use palm sugar for this dish as it gives a rounder, yet more complex flavour.

HASNAH'S BEEF RENDANG

½ kg (1.1 lbs) beef, shoulder or
  round, cut into ½ cm slices
6 dried chillies
6 tablespoons oil
6 shallots, finely sliced
3 cups coconut milk
2 kaffir lime leaves (daun limau
  perut) or grated skin of 1
  kaffir lime
30 g (1 oz) tamarind paste,
  mixed with ¾ cup water and
  ¼ tsp salt

Ground together
4 cloves garlic
5 cm (2 in) ginger
5 red chillies
10 medium-sized shallots,
  finely sliced
2 slices galangal (lengkuas),
  1¼ cm (½ in) each
3 root-ends lemongrass (serai)
½ teaspoon turmeric powder

Cut the dried chillies finely with a pair of scissors.
Pre-heat 6 tablespoons oil in a pan. Fry the cut chillies
till reddish brown, crispy and aromatic. Keep aside for
garnishing.

In the same oil, fry the shallots till golden brown.
Keep aside for garnishing.

With the remaining oil, fry the ground ingredients
until aromatic, then add in half of the coconut milk
followed by the sliced beef. Mix while on a simmer
for five mintes, then include the rest of the milk. Drop
in the kaffir lime leaves or grated skin.

Cook till it begins to thicken then add in half of the
fried dried chillies, ¼ teaspoon salt and tamarind
liquid.

Cook until the meat is tender and the dish is thick.
Toss in a teaspoon or two of sugar according to taste.

Dish out and garnish with the rest of the fried chillies
and fried onions.

AJ's Note: You can also use short ribs if you prefer. You
may combine the lime leaves and grated rinds if you
want a more complex taste.

MY BEEF RENDANG

This is one of my signature dishes where I slow cook the beef, infusing the ingredients and gently bathing the dish with the beef stock. The final tender and flavourful beef is wrapped in fragrant, roasted grated coconut. Do you feel the love?

Ingredients A
1 kg (2.2 lbs) beef, topside, round, shank, cut into 7½ cm (3 in) cubes
4 short ribs
8 shallots, sliced
3 cloves garlic, smashed
1 stalk curry leaf
2 root-ends lemonsgrass (serai) bruised
1 slice galangal (lengkuas), 5 cm (2 in), smashed
1¼ cm (½ in) turmeric, smashed

Blended together
2 root-ends lemongrass (serai)
2½ cm (1 in) ginger
2 large red onions
5 cloves garlic

3 tablespoons oil
4 tablespoons meat curry powder
2½ tablespoons chilli paste
30 g (1 oz) tamarind paste, mixed with ¾ cup water and ¼ tsp salt
1½ cups thick coconut milk
2 star anise
½ teaspoon salt
1 tablespoon palm sugar (gula Melaka)
½ cup fresh grated coconut, pan roasted without oil till golden brown and pounded
1 stalk curry leaves

Half fill a wok with water and bring to the boil. Put in ingredients A and cook slowly over low heat until the beef is tender, about 1 hour. Take out the beef and keep the soup aside for use later.

Heat 3 tablespoons of oil in a saucepan and fry the blended ingredients together with the curry powder and chilli powder.

Put the cooked beef into this curry paste and mix slowly, adding in 4 spoonfuls of the reserved soup, a little at a time.

Mix in the tamarind liquid, coconut milk, star anise, salt and palm sugar, and simmer a while until the beef is nicely mixed with the gravy. Add the roasted coconut. The gravy at this point must be on the thick side. If not, take out the meat and boil down until gravy is of the desired consistancy. Throw in curry leaves.

MILITARY BEEF RENDANG

Uncle Bob Wang was one of my Dad's closest friends in the military. He is a charismatic and deep-voiced man who would always greet my Dad with "Yo Brotherrrrr (rollin the R)" whenever they met. Quoting Uncle Bob: "This is the perfect dish with good friends, steamed rice, salted fish, and a cold beerrrrrr."

1 kg (2.2 lbs) rump steak
5 tablespoons oil
2 tablespoons curry powder
   rendered in 2 tablespoons
   water
½ cup thick coconut milk
½ cup grated fresh coconut,
   fried and ground
3 root-ends lemongrass (serai),
   thinly sliced

Ground together
25 dried chillies, pre-soaked in
   hot water
2 large red onions
4 red chillies
2½ cm (1 in) ginger
2 slices galangal (lengkuas),
   5 cm (2 in) each
5 candlenuts (buah keras)

Mixed together
1 tablespoon soya sauce
1 teaspoon toasted shrimp paste
   (belacan)
1 teaspoon salt
1 tablespoon sugar

Heat oil and fry the ground ingredients and curry powder until fragrant. Add in half of the coconut milk and fry until oil separates.

Add in the soya sauce mix, beef, fried coconut and sliced lemongrass. Fry for 10 minutes, then pour in the rest of the coconut milk. Simmer for 20–25 minutes until the meat is tender.

Increase heat and cook until the oil rises to the top. Check and adjust seasoning according to taste.

S.O.S (SAME OLD STEW)

This is a dish that my best friend Eddie Tang and I will always reminisce about. After a long day of fishing, we tucked into this stew and finished the entire pot meant for six people. It was one of those days where the stew was way better than the fishing.

When my parents are in town, my dad would often say to my mum: "Your son needs his stew." (Yes, I admit I am still my mummy's boy.) To which my mum would reply, "We need to go get some sausages. Andy needs his sausages in his stew." Feeling loved…

½ kg (1.1 lbs) beef, strips, chuck, round
6 sausages, cut into 3, optional
Salt and pepper
Flour for coating beef
Olive oil
2 tablespoons butter
2 large white onions, sliced
8 cloud ear fungus, cut into medium-sized pieces
1 teaspoon dried rosemary
2 bay leaves
1 cinnamon stick
1 star anise
1 chicken cube
1½ tablespoons dark soya sauce
1 medium-sized potato, grated
3 tablespoons Worcestershire sauce
Salt to taste
Sugar to taste

Microwave in water for 12 minutes
2 carrots, cut into bite-sized chunks
3 potatoes, skinned, quartered
2 stalks celery, cut into bite-sized pieces

Cut the beef into 2 in (5 cm) slices and beat with a malet on both sides to tenderise. Season the beef with salt and pepper, and lightly coat with flour.

Heat 4 tablespooons of olive oil and lightly fry the beef, a few at a time, on both sides. Remove the seared beef and set aside.

To the same pan, add in 2 tablespoons of butter, onions, cloud ear fungus, rosemary, bay leaves, cinnamon stick and star anise. Fry together until onions are glassy and the fungus are soft, then add the reserved seared beef.

Pour in enough hot water to cover the beef, then include the chicken cube and dark soya sauce and cook over medium/low heat for about ½ hour or until the meat is cooked and soft. Include the grated potato and mix in well. Add in the sausages here if you are a mummy's boy like me.

Cook for another 10 minutes till the grated potato is soft and dissolving. Now add in the carrots, potatoes, celery and Worcestershire sauce. Check the seasoning and adjust to your taste.

AJ's Note: In my opinion, this dish is incomplete without salted fish, sambal belacan (see page 28) and steaming hot white rice.

BEEF PATTIES IN GRAVY

Beef patties in gravy are just simply divine, eaten as they are, placed on toasted bread or rice, as a topping over pasta, even plated restaurant-style. It is one recipe that is versatile to suit your personal preference.

500 g (1.1 lbs) minced beef
Oil for frying
2 eggs, lightly beaten
1 large red onion, sliced
1 clove garlic, chopped
3 teaspoons cornflour mixed
  with 1 cup water
Salt and pepper to taste
A little black soya sauce for
  colour
1 large tomato, sliced
1 red chilli, seeds removed and
  diced finely for colour

Chopped and add to minced beef
½ large white onion
1 stalk spring onion
5 water chestnuts
5 fresh mushrooms, shitake,
  morels or any mushroom of
  your choice
1 tablespoon cornflour

Mix the meat nicely with the chopped ingredients and form into 6 balls of about billiard ball size, then flatten into patties. You may choose to make larger sized patties if this is your preference.

Heat oil in a frying pan. Dip patties into the egg and fry on both sides. Fry the patties two at a time, taking each batch out when done.

Now fry the remaining egg into an omelette. Remove and set aside.

There should still be a little oil left in the pan. With this, fry the onions until they are soft. Set aside.

Fry the garlic until soft. Pour in the cornflour mixture. Mix well. Season with salt and pepper to taste.

Put back the patties, add in the black soya sauce for colouring, sliced tomatoes and red chillies. Taste and adjust seasoning.

Place the patties onto a dish, arrange tomatoes, omelette and onions over the patties. Pour the remaining sauce over and serve.

MY SAMBAL BELACAN

Although the preferred way to make this sambal is with a motar and pestel, putting all these ingredients in a blender will give you the same sambal in a finer texture.

6 red chillies
4 shallots
6 calamansi (limau kesturi), juiced
1¼ cm (½ in) shrimp paste (belacan) cut widthwise from a 10 x 5 x 5 cm (5 x 2 x 2 in) block, toasted
Rind of one calamansi
1 teaspoon palm sugar (gula Melaka)
⅛ teaspoon salt

Pound or grind all the ingredients together.

AJ's Note: Add in 3-4 bird's eye chillies (chilli padi) if you desire some pain from heat.

BEEF WITH DRIED CHILLIES

½ kg (1.1 lbs) beef, cubed
2 tablespoons oil
8 shallots, sliced finely
4 tomatoes, sliced
6-8 dried chillies, sliced
4 tablespoons sweet dark soya sauce
2 cups coconut milk
3 cloves
¼ grated nutmeg or ⅙ teaspoon nutmeg powder
2½ cm (1 in) cinnamon stick
Salt and sugar to taste
Fried onions
Almonds or cashewnuts

Blended together
4 coves garlic
3 candlenuts (buah keras), roasted
2 cm (¾ in) ginger

Heat the oil and fry the shallots till soft, then add in the blended ingredients and fry until fragrant. Put in the sliced tomatoes, dried chillies and beef, and stir nicely until the beef is well coated.

Mix in the sweet dark soya sauce, then slowly add in the coconut milk, stirring while doing so. Now put in the cloves, grated nutmeg and cinnamon.

Lower the heat and cook until the beef is tender and oil separates from the gravy. Season to taste. Sprinkle on the fried onions, almonds or cashewnuts as garnish.

AJ's Note: Use more or less dried chillies depending on how spicey you want your dish to be.

PASANDA BEEF

450 g (1 lb) beef, chuck, flank,
  topside, stew meat, cut into
  2½ cm (1 in) strips
3 tablespoons oil
2 large red onions, chopped
2 tablepoons chilli paste
4 green chillies
Juice of ½ lemon
1 teaspoon palm sugar
  (gula Melaka)
Coriander leaves, chopped
Almond flakes

Marinade
4 tablespoons Greek yoghurt
2½ teaspoons coriander powder
1½ teaspoons cumin powder
4 candlenuts (buah keras) or
  almonds, pounded
1 teaspoon garam masala
3 cloves garlic, chopped
5 cm (2 in) ginger, chopped
Salt to taste

Mix the meat and the marinade in a bowl. Leave to marinate for at least 4 hours.

Heat oil and fry onions until well browned. Add in the marinated meat and chilli paste and fry until all ingredients are well mixed and infused. Add in 1 cup hot water and green chillies. Cover and slow cook on low heat until meat is tender.

Now put in a the lemon juice and palm sugar. Check and adjust salt according to taste. Garnish with chopped coriander leaves and flaked almonds.

AJ's Notes: This is a classic dish that was traditionally prepared with lamb – if you love lamb, you should try it with lamb. It can also be prepared with chicken and king prawns. Should you opt for chicken or prawns, the addition of hot water is reduced to ½ cup, as chicken and prawns cook faster than lamb or beef.

SPICY BEEF MADRAS

1 kg (2.2 lbs) beef, top side,
    rump, cubed, or short ribs
1 cup grated fresh coconut
1 tin (400 g, 14 oz) tomatoes
2 tablespoons grated ginger
2 teaspoons mustard seeds
15 g (½ oz) tamarind paste,
    mixed with ¼ cup water
2 tablespoons oil
3 large red onions, chopped
2 cloves garlic, chopped
3 sprigs curry leaf
Grated skin of 1 kaffir lime
½ cup water
5-6 mint leaves for garnish

Ground spices
1 teaspoon turmeric powder
2 tablespoons coriander powder
2 teaspoons chilli powder
1 tablespoon ground cumin

Blend together the coconut, undrained tomatoes, ginger, mustard seeds and tamarind. Set aside. (This will be referred to later as the coconut mix.)

Pre-heat oil, cook onions and garlic, stirring until lightly browned. Add in the ground spices and cook until fragrant.

Add in the curry leaves, beef, grated kaffir lime skin, water and coconut mix. Simmer covered for about 1½ hours, stirring occasionally until beef is tender.

Garnish with mint leaves when ready to serve. Lime pickle (page 16) is a condiment served with this dish.

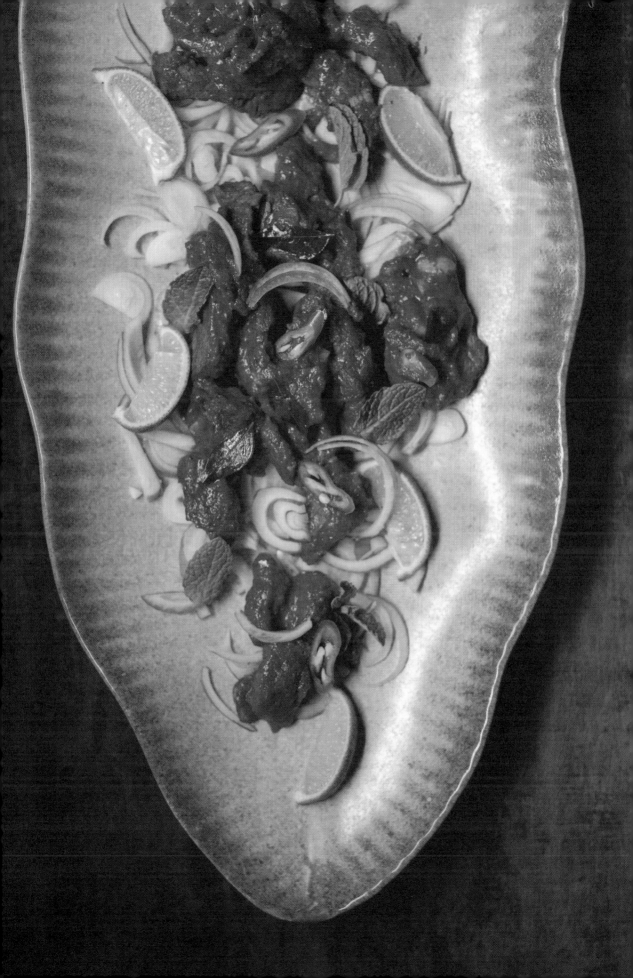

SATAY

I would say this is the simplest dish to prepare. Everything goes into a blender to make a fragrant and flavourful marinade for meat to be grilled.

½ kg (1.1 lbs) lean beef, chicken or pork
4 tablespoons thick coconut milk

Ground together
1 clove garlic
5 cm (2 in) fresh ginger
4 shallots
1 teaspoon coriander seeds
1 teaspoon turmeric powder
8 dried chillies
½ teaspoon black peppercorns
3 root-ends lemongrass (serai)
1½ tablespoons plam sugar (gula Melaka) or brown sugar

Use the smoothly-ground paste to marinate the meat. Refrigerate overnight.

Mix the coconut milk with the marinated meat.

Skewer the meat and grill over coals till chared and tender.

AJ's Notes: The same marinade can also be used on chicken drumsticks, drumlettes, chicken wings, pork belly, pork ribs or spare ribs, beef ribs and short ribs. So, explore, and let your creativity flow.

Traditionally, satay is served with satay sauce, and I have included this recipe below for you as well.

SATAY SAUCE

2 cups roasted unsalted peanuts, coarsely pounded
¼ cup peanut oil
30 g (1 oz) tamarind paste, mixed with ¾ cup water and ¼ tsp salt
1½ tablespoons palm sugar (gula Melaka)
¼ cup thick coconut milk

Blended together
8 dried red chilies, pre-soaked in warm water before blending
3 cloves garlic
6 shallots
2 root-ends lemongrass (serai)
2 slices galangal (lengkuas), 1¼ cm (½ in) each
1 tablespoon coriander

Pre-heat a pan with ¼ cup peanut oil, and fry the blended ingredients until aromatic.

Once fragrant, add in the peanuts, tamarind juice, palm sugar and gently stir in the mixture. Allow to simmer on low heat, gently stirring for about 5 minutes.

Now add in the coconut milk and continue to simmer for 15-20 minutes until you notice the peanut sauce has a smooth yet chunky texture. It is natural to also see a layer of oil form above the sauce as the oil separates from the peanuts and coconut milk.

BEEF STEW

I love slow cooking as it's simple and the gentle heat cooks your food to perfection. The marriage of high-tech cooking with century-old cooking principles in a crock pot enables the extraction of an abundance of flavours.

½ kg (1.1 lb) beef, cubed
1 daikon (Chinese radish)
½ tablespoon sesame oil
3 cups water
2 cups clear chicken stock
1 tablespoon sugar
4 tablespoons Chinese rice wine
  or Yomeishu
½ cup clear chicken stock

Ingredients A
4 tablespoons oil
3 cloves garlic, chopped
5 cm (2 in) young ginger, sliced
½ large white onion, sliced
3 star aniseed

Cut the diakon into bite-sized pieces and soak in water mixed with 1 teaspoon of sesame oil for 10 minutes.

Pour the water, 2 cups of chicken stock and the sugar into a crock pot. Give it a few stirs and leave it.

Pre-heat oil and fry garlic, ginger, onion and aniseed lightly for about 2-3 minutes. Add beef, Chinese rice wine (or Yomeishu) and ½ cup chicken stock, and bring it to a boil.

Once boiling, switch off heat and transfer into the crock-pot. Add in the daikon. Cover and stew for 5 hours on high.

AJ's Notes: This recipe takes only 15 minutes to prepare prior to cooking in the crock pot. For the working adult, preparing this in the morning and setting the crock-pot to slow cook for 8 hours will result in a beautiful and savory dinner when you get home.

To prepare this dish for mums during their confinement period, replace the chicken stock with Brands Essence of Chicken and be sure to use Yomeishu.

OXTAIL CASSEROLE

My sister Barbara and I will always have a good laugh when we think about this dish. We must have been 8-9 years old when we first had this, and while being served we both said, "Can we have the small pieces?" To which my grandmother replied, "But the larger pieces have more meat?" We looked at each other and my sister said, "Grandma, the larger pieces are closest to the cow's bum!"

1.5 kg (3.3 lbs) large oxtail
½ teaspoon salt
¾ teaspoon black pepper
2 large white onions, diced
1 carrot, diced
1 small green pepper, diced
1 stalk celery, diced
3 slices bacon, diced
4 tablespoons flour for coating meat
2 chicken cubes
2 bay leaves
Black soya sauce
Salt, sugar and pepper to taste
3 teaspoons cornflour mixed with 1 cup water
Worcestershire sauce
Oil

Cut the oxtail into joints and soak in water for about 1 hour. Take out and set aside.

Season the oxtail joints with ½ teaspoon salt and ¾ teaspoon black pepper, then sprinkle on about 4 tablespoons of flour to coat the meat.

Coat the pan with 10 tablespoons oil and fry the oxtail joints a few at a time in a non-stick pan until golden.

Remove oil, leaving about 3 tablespoons to fry all the diced ingredients together. When soft, add in 5 cups of boiling water, chicken cubes, bay leaf and oxtail joints.

Allow to boil slowly for about 20 minutes then transfer to a pressure cooker to cook for 15 minutes until soft. Should the pressure cooker not be available, continue the slow boil for an additional 20-25 minutes.

Add in the black sauce, salt, pepper and sugar to taste and thicken with cornflour mixture to further thicken the gravy. Finally, put in a few shakes of Worcestershire sauce.

Serve on buttered pasta (sphaghetti, linguine, penne) or mashed potatoes.

PARSLEY-FLAVOURED KEBABS

2 rib eye steaks (1.6 kg, 3.5 lbs),
   cut into 2 x 2 cm (1 x 1 in)
   cubes
Fresh pineapples, wedged
1 yellow capsicum, wedged
10 shallots, skinned
Zest of 1 lemon
Pinch of cinnamon powder

Marinade
3 cloves garlic
2 tablespoons red wine vinegar
1 sprig coriander leaves, chopped
1 teaspoon sugar
Salt to taste
Black pepper to taste
1 teaspoon chilli flakes
½ cup olive oil

Pulse all marinade ingredients until smooth. Divide mixture into two.

Use one portion of the mixture to marinate the beef. Refrigerate overnight. Keep the remaining marinade.

The next day, skewer two pieces of beef among one piece each of the pineapple, capsicum and onion.

Grate the zest from one lemon and a pinch of cinnamon powder and add it to the second portion of marinade.

Baste nicely with the lemon and cinnamon marinade and grill, 4–5 minutes on each side.

AJ's Notes: Tenderloin, top sirloin, tender medallions are alternative cuts. This same recipe can also be prepared with chicken or lamb. If lamb is used, add the following into the marinade: 1 stick of rosemary leaves (stem removed), 8 mint leaves and 1 teaspoon coriander powder.

RED BEEF CURRY

Directly translated, the Malay name of this dish — Daging Simerah Saga — refers to the curry's colour, red like the seeds of the Saga Tree (Adenanthera pavonina), also known as the red coral tree. Native to India, the seeds were used to weigh gold — 4 seeds to one gram of gold. The word 'saga' can also be traced to an Arabic term for goldsmith.

Growing up, there were many games we played using these seeds. Chongkak (a count and capture game) and five stones (similar to jacks) were common, but my personal favourite was the bean bag filled with seeds collected from my Uncle Earl's garden. Believe me, there is no beanbag like a saga seed beanbag!

1 kg (2.2 lbs) beef, topside, round, shank, cut into 7½ cm (3 in) cubes
150 g (5 oz) clarified butter (ghee)
2 pandan leaves, knotted
¼ teaspoon nutmeg powder
1½ tablespoons chilli paste
1 cup coconut milk
3 tablespoons tomato paste
½ cup evaporated milk
Salt and sugar to taste

Blended together
1 whole pod garlic
2 large red onions
5 cm (2 in) ginger
2 slices galangal (lengkuas), 5 cm (2 in) each

Spice mix
6 cloves
3 whole star anise
5 cm (2 in) cinnamon stick
4 cardamoms

Garnish
Green peas
Coriander leaves, chopped
Fried shallots

Fry the blended ingredients in the clarified butter together with the spice mix, pandan leaves and grated nutmeg. When fragrant, add in the meat, chilli paste, coconut milk and tomato paste. Mix well and continue to simmer.

When the meat is soft, add in the evaporated milk and season with salt and sugar to taste. Stir thoroughly. Dish up and garnish with green peas, coriander leaves and fried shallots.

ORANGE BEEF FILLETS ON HOT PLATE

250 g (½ lb) beef fillet, sliced
4 tablespoons oil
½ large white onion
3 red chillies
1 red, yellow or green capsicum
½ tablespoon Chinese rice wine
Slices of orange for garnishing

Marinade
1 tablespoon light soya sauce
1 teaspoon dark soya
½ teaspoon sugar
½ teaspoon sesame oil
½ teaspoon white pepper
1½ teaspoon cornflour

Sauce
¼ teaspoon salt
1½ teaspoon sugar
5 tablespoons orange juice
1 teaspoon orange zest
½ orange, skinned and wedged

Mix the marinade ingredients and use it to marinate the beef for 15 minutes.

Shallow fry the beef in oil till medium doneness. Dish out and keep aside.

Remove most of the oil, leaving 1 tablespoon. Fry the onion in this until fragrant. Now add in the chillies and capsicum and fry for another minute.

Add the beef in the mixture, put in the Chinese wine, and stir well. Switch off heat and set aside.

Heat up the hot plate or griddle pan then put beef mix into it.

In a separate pan, heat up 1 tablespoon of cooking oil and stir in the sauce ingredients. Pour over beef in hot plate or griddle pan. Garnish with orange slices. Serve in hot plate or griddle pan

BAKED MINCED BEEF ON LEMONGRASS

This dish started as Sugar Cane Beef as when I created it, I used sugar cane sticks. It gives the dish a very unique flavour and chewing on the sugar cane sticks after your meal leaves refreshing sweetness on your palate. As sugar cane is not readily available (although always my first choice), I opted to use lemongrass stalks after visiting Bali in the early 1990s.

10 stalks of lemongrass, wiped with a damp cloth and slightly bruised
500g (1 lb) minced beef

Blended together
2 large red onions
5 cloves garlic
5 cm (2 in) young ginger
2 kaffir lime leaves

Mixture A
1½ tablespoons chilli paste
1 tablespoon sesame oil
1 teaspoon salt
1 egg
1 tablespoon tomato puree
8 shallots, sliced
2 stalks spring onions, chopped
¾ teaspoon turmeric powder

Mixture B
2 tomatoes, deseeded and diced
1 red and 1 green chilli, seeds removed, chillies diced finely
4 shallots, diced finely
½ tablespoons apple vinegar

For basting
4 tablespoons olive oil
1 teaspoon sesame oil
2 tablespoons sweet soy sauce (kicap manis)
1 teaspoon palm sugar (gula Melaka)

Place minced beef in a large bowl. Add in blended ingredients and mixture A. Stir in well and leave to marinade for 1-2 hours.

Shape the marinated meat mixture around the lemongrass stalks. Pre-heat the oven to 200°C (400°F). Thereafter, place the sticks of meat on a tray, apply one coat of the baste and place in oven. Turn after 15 minutes, baste again and continue to cook for another 10 minutes. Place on a serving dish and sprinkle with the chopped spring onions.

Pour the remaining mixture for basting into a bowl, and add in mixture B. This can be used as a dip for the lemongrass beef sticks or spooned on top before serving.

AJ's Notes: Bruising the ends of the lemongrass stalks will enable the meat to hold better onto the stalks, and the flavour of the lemongrass will infuse into the meat.

DAD'S SHEPHERDS PIE

If you ask me what comfort food is to me, this is one of them. One of my Dad's specialiaties, this recipe triggers memories of my cooking for the first time, guided by Dad. Although we did not prepare Shepherd's Pie, I somehow associate it with the first time I handled a ladle and a wok to cook my first dish.

½ kg (1.1 lb) beef mince
3 tablespoons oil
5 cm (2 in) cinnamon stick
1 star anise
3 cloves
1 large onion white, chopped
1 cup bacon bits
1 sprig rosemary or 1 teaspoon
   rosemary powder
2 bay leaves
1 red chilli, cut finely
2 tablespoons oyster sauce
1 teaspoon dark soya sauce
2 medium-sized potatoes, diced
1 large carrot, diced
1 stalk celery, diced
Salt and pepper to taste
Sugar to taste
1 cup mint leaves
4 large potatoes, boiled and
   mashed
1 cup grated cheddar cheese

Heat oil and fry the cinnamon, star anise and cloves to flavour the oil. Put in the chopped onions and bacon bits. Stir to cook till the onions are glassy.

Include the beef mince, rosemary sprig, bay leaves and chilli. Stir well. Allow to cook for a few minutes then add in the oyster sauce and dark soya sauce. Pour in 1 cup of hot water, cover the pan, and simmer for about 10 minutes.

Now add in the diced potatoes, carrot and celery and continue to cook until the potato softens. Season with salt, pepper and a little sugar. Drop in mint leaves and stir. Switch off fire.

Preheat an oven to 175°C (350°F). Remove the mince mixture to a baking dish. Cover mince evenly with the mashed potatoes, sprinkle cheese over and bake until golden.

AJ's Notes: The best way to make your own bacon bits is to slice fresh bacon into ½ cm slices. You need not separate them. However, washing them before cooking is essential to remove excess fat and salt. Place into a clean saucepan. Use medium-high heat to slow cook the bacon. You are looking at a 20 minute cooking time. Once you see a layer of froth over the bacon it will be almost ready. Stir to reduce the frothing. Strain once the right texture of crispness is acquired to separate the bacon bits from the bacon oil. The bacon oil can be kept to use in a salad dressing or to make scrambled eggs.

For those who prefer the oven, the bacon is flattened out on a tray and placed into a pre-heated oven of 175°C (350°F) degrees. Leave in for 20 minutes, and remove them once you see that the bacon is a dark golden brown.

GOAN MEAT CURRY

I wrote this recipe after I visited the spice markets in Goa when I was in my mid-twenties. Goan cuisine has predominantly fish, seafood, purees and pickle dishes, so tasting Sarapatel – a meat dish of Portugese origin – gave me an idea.

I call it 'meat curry' as it can be prepared with lamb, beef or chicken, or sometimes all three meats. I have fond memories of the Anjuna market and the spice 'heaven' of Ponda, the purity of the land and the people who care for it.

500 g (1.1 lbs) lamb
500 g (1.1 lbs) lean beef
115 g (2 oz) clarified butter
   (ghee) or 4 tablespoons olive
   oil
1 large red onion, chopped
5 cloves garlic, chopped
5 cloves garlic, ground to a paste
2½ cm (1 in) young ginger,
   ground to a paste
½ teaspoon ground tumeric
3 green chillies, deseeded and
   chopped
2 teaspoon aniseed powder
   (jintan manis)
½ teaspoon salt
¼ cup coconut milk
1 cup hot water
3 sprigs coriander leaves, chopped

Heat the clarified butter in a pan and fry chopped onion and garlic until light brown. Add in garlic paste, ginger paste, turmeric, green chillies and meat and mix well. Fry until the meat is coated and ingredients are infused to the meat.

Sprinkle in the aniseed powder, salt and slowly stir in coconut cream. Continue to stir fry for 5 minutes.

Add in 1 cup hot water and coriander leaves. Give it a quick mix and cover the pot and simmer on low heat for a further 25-30 minutes until meat is tender.

AJ's Notes: If you are using chicken, you only need to simmer for 10-15 minutes as chicken cooks much faster than red meats.

Lime pickle (page 16) is a condiment eaten with this dish when served with Roti Canai or Purees.

GAYLYNN'S SIZZLING BEEF

This is a classic Thai-inspired beef salad. Simple, yet so delicate in aroma and flavors.

½ kg (1.1 lbs) beef, cubed or cut
    into strips
3 tablespoons olive oil
Chilli flakes, optional
Juice from 1 calamansi lime
    (limau kesturi), optional

Blended together
½ bunch coriander with roots
2 red chillies
5 cm (2 in) young ginger
Juice from 2 large fresh limes
2 cloves garlic
2 tablespoons fish sauce
1 tablespoon palm sugar
    (gula Melaka)

Raw Ingredients
6 shallots, thinly sliced
1 red chilli, finely sliced
½ cup mint leaves
½ cup Thai sweet basil leaves
8 coriander leaves
¼ cup chopped almonds
¼ teaspoon black pepper
¼ teaspoon salt

Mix half of the blended ingredients in a bowl with the beef. Allow to marinate for 1-2 hours. Once ready, pre-heat a pan with olive oil, fry the beef until it is seared and slightly crisp on the tips.

Place all the beef into a mixing bowl, add in the remaining blended ingredients and the raw ingredients.

Toss and mix well, adding the chilli flakes and lime juice if using. The dish is ready to be served.

CAVEMAN BEEF NOODLES

This is a quick and dirty (hence 'caveman') recipe to use with any type of noodles. Flat rice noodles (koay teow) is my personal preference.

500 g (1.1 lbs) beef, strips or
    topside
2 tablespoons oil
½ large white onion, chopped
2 dried red chillies, cut into
    small pieces, optional
2 inch (5 cm) young ginger,
    grated
3 cloves garlic, crushed
2 tablespoons sweet chilli sauce
1 tablespoon dark soya sauce
1 tablespoon light soya sauce
1 tablespoon oyster sauce
1 teaspoon goji berry (wolfberry)
1 red capsicum, diced
1 cup beansprouts, cleaned
2 teaspoons cornflour mixed in
    ¼ cup water
1 sprig coriander leaves, chopped

Noodles
200 g (7 oz) noodles
1 tablespoon oil
2 tablespoons black rice vinegar

Beef
Cut the beef into 2 in (5 cm) slices and beat with a mallet on both sides to tenderise. Season the beef with salt and black pepper.

Heat oil in pan, add in onion, dried chilli, ginger and garlic. Stir fry until onion is soft. Add in beef strips and stir in until beef is lightly browned.

Stir in all sauces, gojiberry, capsicum and beansprouts and cook until capsicum softens. Add in cornflour mixture and coriander leaves and stir till gravy thickens.

Noodles
Blanch the noodles (this will cook them about 90 percent). In a wok, heat up 1 tablespoon of oil. Turn the flame high and put in blanched noodles. This will sear the noodles, removing any water. Once the noodles are dry, add in the black vinegar. Turn off the fire and toss. This gives the noodles a slight, seared black vinegar flavour.

Portion noodles on individual plates and pour over the prepared beef. Serve.

CHICKEN

COCONUT CHICKEN

Simplicity is often the first principle in making a great dish. Coconut water is sacred in some cultures as the water is pure and un-touched by man. This dish was inspired by a Hindu friend when we were watching the Thaipusam procession in Penang. The devotees were smashing coconuts on the roads to symbolise "the breaking of one's ego to reveal purity inside".

1 chicken, approximately 1.5 kg (3.3 lbs), skinned and cut into 12 pieces
8 tablespoons clarified butter (ghee) or oil
1 large red onion, sliced
2 cloves garlic, sliced
1 teaspoon salt
Flesh of 1 young coconut, thinly sliced
1½ tablespoons tomato paste
1 cup coconut water
1 teaspoon sugar

Spice mix
4 cardamoms
4 cloves
2½ cm (1 in) cinnamon stick
2 teaspoons garam masala
1 teaspoon turmeric powder
2 tablespoons chilli powder

Melt ghee in pan and fry the onions and garlic until soft. Put in the spice mix and salt, and then the chicken pieces.

Fry well until the chicken is brown, then add in the coconut, tomato paste and coconut water. Stir and bring to the boil.

Lower heat, cover and simmer until the chicken is done, about 20 minutes. Finally, add in the sugar.

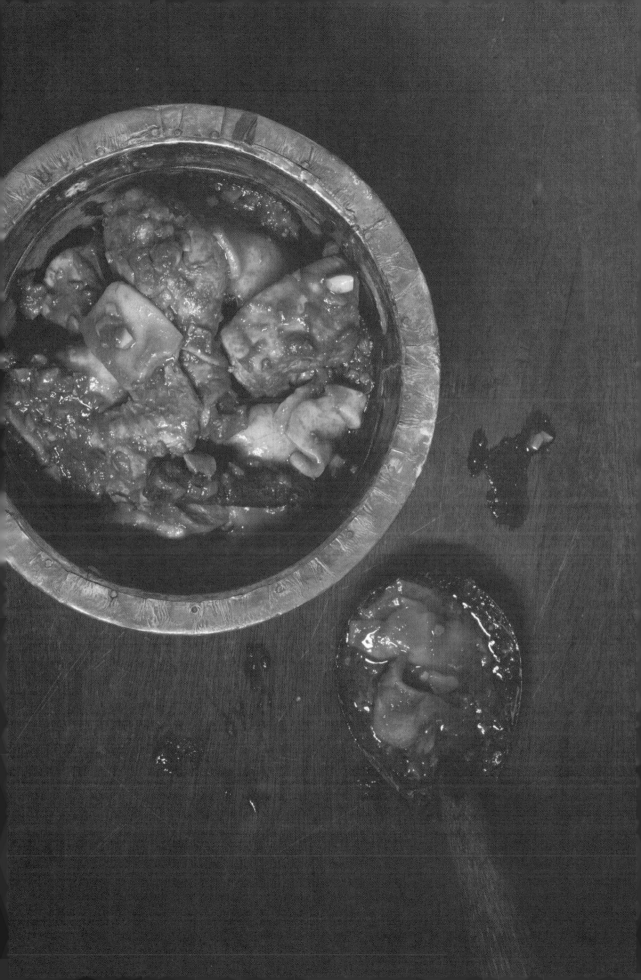

KAFFIR LIME CHICKEN

Citrus hystrix, commonly known in English as kaffir lime is, in my opinion, a magical element in Asian cuisine. The leaves and fruit offer a scent which no other "lime" leaf can offer. Whenever I think of this dish, I am reminded by the old classic Malay teka-teki or riddle where they ask "Daun-nya kret met mot, buah-nya kret tet tot – apa saya?" (My leaf is strangely shaped, my fruit is like a brain – what am I?) And the answer would be "Daun Limau Purut and Buah Limau Purut." (Kaffir Lim leaf and fruit). This is something I am sure many of my Malaysian friends who cook will relate to with a smile...

1 chicken, approximatly 1.5 kg (3.3 lbs), cut into 12 pieces
1 ping-pong-ball sized tamarind paste rendered in ½ cup water
¾ teaspoon salt

Oil for frying
3-5 kaffir lime leaves (daun limau perut), shredded
1 cup thick coconut milk
¼ cup thick coconut milk mixed with ¼ cup hot water

Ground together
4 slices galangal (lengkuas)
7 dried chillies
3 fresh chillies
10 white peppercorns
4 cloves garlic
6 shallots
2½ teaspoons coriander seeds
1½ teaspoons cumin seeds
1 root-end lemongrass (serai)
1½ cm (½ in) fresh turmeric (kunyit)
4 candlenuts (buah keras)
1 slice ginger
4 cm (1½ in) palm sugar (gula Melaka)

Season chicken with the tamarind liquid and salt. Leave for about 15 minutes.

Heat oil and fry the ground ingredients until aromatic. Add in the kaffir lime leaves, thick coconut milk and chicken to fry in the mixture, turning the chicken a few times to coat it well. Pour in the diluted coconut milk and mix well. Taste and adjust seasoning. Transfer the chicken into a dish and pour over the gravy from the frying.

Bake in a moderate oven of 150°C (302°F) for about 30 minutes or until done. Remove. Pour the gravy over the chicken and serve.

Top: Kaffir Lime Chicken
Bottom: Pork Lemongrass Curry
(page 143)

CHICKEN BREASTS IN BASIL

My bodybuilding friends (or "FitFam" as they are affectionately known) often ask me to come up with dishes that rebut the notion that eating 'clean' is boring. Here is one that they love.

4 chicken breasts, sliced
   horizontally and butterflied
1 cup fresh basil leaves,
   chopped
2 cloves garlic, chopped
¼ cup pine nuts or chopped
   almonds, toasted
½ cup extra virgin olive oil or
   flaxseed oil
2 tablespoons organic balsamic
   vinegar
Himalayan Pink Salt to taste,
   optional
Cracked black pepper to taste
12 pineapple wedges
Wedges of lemon, optional

Place basil, garlic, nuts, oil, vinegar, salt and pepper in a bowl. Stir to combine to make a dressing.

Place the chicken in a non-metallic dish and pour in half the dressing over it. Massage into meat then Cover and refrigerate for 1 hour.

Heat a non-stick pan and cook the chicken with the pineapple for 4 minutes on each side. Serve with the remaining dressing. Offer wedges of lemon to diners to squeeze on if they so prefer.

AJ's Notes: Thai sweet basil is preferred for this dish. Vinegars are one of the oldest traditional health foods found throughout the world. Organic or natural vinegars have health properties because they retain the health characteristics of the fruit they were fermented from – without the sugar.

ROASTED SESAME CHICKEN

1 medium-sized chicken,
    approximately 1.5 kg (3.3lbs)
3 tablespoons brown sugar
1 teaspoon salt
3 tablespoons sesame seeds for
    coating chicken

Marinade
1½ tablespoon honey
2 tablespoons black rice vinegar
2 tablespoon sesame oil
1 teaspoon sea salt

For gravy
2 tablespoons sesame oil
2 tablespoons black rice vinegar
1 tablespoon honey

Rub the inside of the chicken with the brown sugar and sea salt. Keep aside for half hour.

Massage the marinade of honey, vinegar, sesame oil and sea salt on the skin of the chicken. Slip your seasonings under the skin to get full flavor and moist meat especially on the breast area, gently pushing the mix under the skin without tearing it.

Sprinkle the sesame seeds over the chicken, covering it moderately. Hang the prepared chicken up to dry for an hour.

Always put the chicken into a preheated oven 230°C (450°F) and thereafter lower the heat and cook at the correct temperature 180°C (356°F).

Place the chicken on a rack over a tray to catch the dripping. This juice is the foundation of a great sauce.

I prefer to roast the underside for the first 15–20 minutes until it begins to brown before turning over the chicken to the breast side to slowly cook it for a further 40 minutes or to the point where you see the skin becoming crisp. Occasionally baste the chicken with the marinade while it is cooking

Once the chicken is cooked, take out and set aside. Pour in ½ cup of hot water into the tray with the juices, mix well and pour out into a sauce pan. Now add in the sesame oil, black rice vinegar and honey for the gravy and stir well. Bring to the boil and the gravy is ready to be served with your roast chicken.

AJ's Note: If the sesame seeds begin to brown or blacken before the chicken is cooked, it means that your oven is too hot.

AYAM PADANG

*Food from Padang, the city on the western coast of Sumatra, Indonesia, is famous for its rich taste of coconut milk, spicy chilli and heavy spice mixtures. This is typical of Minangkabau cuisine which shows distinctive Indian and Middle Eastern influences. What I enjoy most about the cuisine is that every one of its variety of dishes (*hidangan *in Indonesian) has a unique taste to tantalize your tastebuds, from the rich, coconut-milk-infused rendang to the tongue-numbing chilli that results in sweat....*

1 chicken, approximately 1.5 kg (3.3 lbs), cut into 8 pieces
4 tablespoons oil
3 tablespoons chilli paste
2 cinnamon sticks, 7½ cm (3 in) each
3 star anise
1½ cups thick coconut milk
½ teaspoon salt
¾ teaspoon palm sugar (gula Melaka)
2 slices dried 'tamarind' (assam gelugor, assam keping)
1 large turmeric leaf, remove midrib and tear each side into 4 pieces

Wet spices
3 root-ends lemongrass (serai)
2 large red onions
5 cm (2 in) ginger
5 cm (2 in) turmeric (kunyit) or ¾ teaspoon turmeric powder
2½ cm (1 in) galangal (lengkuas)
5 candlenuts (buah keras)
1 teaspoon grated nutmeg
3 cloves garlic

Blend the wet spices to a puree and keep aside.

Heat oil and fry the blended ingredients with the chilli paste, cinnamon and star anise until fragrant.

While simmering, add in the chicken and stir until the chicken pieces are coated. While turning the chicken pieces, slowly pour in the coconut milk and mix well.

Now add the salt and palm sugar, then the 'tamarind' slices and turmeric leaf. Stir and allow to slow cook on medium heat for approximately 20 minutes until the chicken is done.

AJ's Note: If you prefer dark meat, use 8 chicken thighs for this dish.

HAWAIIAN BBQ CHICKEN

This is yet another favourite that I created for my "FitFam" bodybuilding friends. It's a recipe for those who want to eat clean and have an abundance of natural flavours in their food. Pak Halim Haron, Ray Razak, Syabil, Cody, Ray Yoe, Rinn Farina, Hapsari Marsden, Yvonne and Jia, this one is for you, with love.

6 chicken breasts or 6 chicken
   thighs if you prefer dark meat
3 tablespoons olive oil
1 sweet pineapple, grated
¾ cup thick coconut milk
Salt and pepper to taste

Spice mix
2 tablespoons coriander powder
2 tablespoons chilli powder
   mixed in ½ cup warm water
½ tablespoons turmeric (kunyit)
   powder

Blended together
1 young ginger, approximately
   150g, (5 oz)
6 cloves garlic
6 shallots
1 root-end lemongrass (serai)
6 fresh chillies

Prepare the spice mix, combine with the blended ingredients and fry in oil for 5 minutes. Add in the grated pineapple and simmer for 10 mins over low heat.

Put in the coconut milk and season with salt and pepper to taste. Leave to cool

Marinate the chicken with this sauce for at least 3 hours and barbecue or grill on a griddle pan.

AJ's Notes: For the best result, do not use the coconut cream that comes in a tin or a pack. Use pure coconut cream extracted from a freshly grated coconut. Soak 2 cups of freshly grated coconut in 1 cup of warm water for about 10 minutes. Blend it in a blender for 30 seconds, wrap it in a muslin cloth and squeeze the pulp to extract the fresh coconut milk.

SPUTNIK CHICKEN (RIGHT)

Sputnik was the first man-made satellite launched in 1957 by the Soviet Union. You could say I went into orbit after having this dish.

1 chicken, approximately 1.5 kg (3.3 lbs), cut into 8 pieces
3 tablespoons palm sugar (gula Melaka)
3 tablespoons vinegar
2 tablespoons dark soya
1 cup light soya sauce
4 tablespoons olive oil
12 shallots, blended
1½ tablespoons chilli paste
¾ cup almonds or cashew nuts, lightly crushed or halved
Juice from 2 calamansi limes

Marinate chicken pieces with the palm sugar, vinegar, dark soya sauce and plenty of light soya sauce (this will finally be the gravy). Keep aside and marinate for 1 to 2 hours.

Heat up olive oil and fry the chicken pieces, keeping the marinade aside.

Remove all but 3 tablespoons of oil and fry the shallots and chilli paste until fragrant.

Return the chicken to the saucepan together with the reserved marinade and further cook until the chicken is well coated with the marinade. Check and adjust seasoning to taste. Finally, add in the nuts and calamansi juice and mix well.

DAD'S MASALA YOGHURT CHICKEN

1 chicken, approximately 1.5 kg (3.3 lbs), skinned and cut into 10 serving pieces
4 tablespoons oil
1 large red onion, sliced
2 root-ends lemongrass (serai), bruised
1 teaspoon chopped garlic
2½ cm (1 in) ginger, sliced
½ teaspoon ground black pepper
2 teaspoons chilli paste
2 teaspoons turmeric powder
1 cup coriander leaves, chopped
2 teaspoons garam masala
270 g (9.5 oz) yoghurt
2 green chillies, halved lengthwise
Salt and sugar to taste
Coriander leaves

Fry the onions in the oil together with the bruised lemongrass. When the onions become soft, add in the garlic and ginger and fry until they are light golden.

Add in the chicken pieces, mix well, then add the pepper, chilli paste, turmeric powder, coriander leaves and garam masala. Turn the chicken to seal meat for 10 minutes. This sealing process will also infuse the ingredients with the chicken.

Now, add boiling water to just about cover the chicken and simmer for an additional 10 minutes. Thereafter, stir while adding in the yoghurt a spoon at a time, followed by the green chillies, and salt and sugar to taste.

Cook until chicken is done. Garnish with a few sprigs of coriander leaves.

CHICKEN MASALA

Masala is a mixture of ground spices used in Indian, Persian and Middle-Eastern cuisine. It is a fact that these spices are considered 'heaty' in the sense of it raising body metabolism which differ from chillies which just make you perspire. My mouth waters when I think about this dish.

1 chicken or parts, approximately
   1.5 kg (3.3 lbs)
1 teaspoon salt
1 teaspoon turmeric powder
4 tablespoons oil
2 large red onions, chopped
1 teaspoon pepper
1 tablespoon palm sugar (gula Melaka)

Ground together
4 green chillies
4 teaspoons coriander seeds
3 sprigs coriander leaves
1 teaspoon cumin seeds
6 cloves garlic
½ cup grated coconut
2 cloves
5 curry leaves
1 bay leaf
2½ cm (1 in) cinnamon stick
2 cardamoms
¼ teaspoon fenugreek seeds
   (halba)
¼ teaspoon mustard seeds
¼ teaspoon grated nutmeg
2½ cm (1 in) ginger

Garnish
1 large tomato, seeded and diced
1 green chilli, sliced
1½ teaspoon chopped almonds
   or cashew nuts
Coriander leaves, chopped

Season the chicken with salt and turmeric. Keep aside.

Heat the oil and fry onions till they are glassy and slightly brown, then add in the ground ingredients (masala) and fry until brown and aromatic.

Add in chicken and mix till the chicken is evenly coated. Pour in 1 cup of water and cook on low/medium heat, occasionally stirring to bring the ingredients on the bottom to the top, until done.

Season with pepper and add the sugar. Mix well. Garnish with diced tomatoes, sliced green chillies, nuts and coriander leaves.

MALAY-STYLE CHICKEN

One of the oldest Malay style recipes I learnt while growing up, this was traditionally prepared with a batu giling. *Using this grindstone is, in my opinion, the best way to make spices into a paste with a consistent texture. In modern times, a spice grinder is preferred when small amounts are required.*

1 chicken, approximately 1.5kg (3.3 lbs), cut into 12 serving pieces
1 tablespoon turmeric powder (kunyit)
1 tablespoon black pepper
½ tablespoon white pepper
4 tablespoons oil
15 dried chillies, lightly fried in 2 tablespoons oil, ground
2 tablespoons black sweet soya sauce
4 large white onions, sliced into rings
12 cloves, soaked in water
5 cm (2 in) cinnamon stick, soaked in water
1 whole star anise, soaked in water
4 stalks curry leaves
1 ping-pong-ball-sized tamarind paste rendered in ½ cup water

Ingredients A, ground together
1½ in (7cm) fresh ginger
3 slices galangal (lengkuas)
2 root-ends lemongrass (serai)
5 cloves garlic
2 large red onions

Ground together
1 tablespoon fennel (jintan manis)
1 tablespoon cumin (jintan putih)

Garnish
1 diced green chilli, deseeded

Season the chicken pices with the turmeric, black and white pepper and shallow fry in the 4 tablespoons of oil until golden.

In the same oil, fry the ground ingredients A, then add in the ground chillies and the ground fennel and cummin. Fry until fragrant.

Put in the chicken, stir well, then add the sweet black soya sauce and the sliced onions. Simmer until the onions soften. Now put in the soaked spices (cloves,, cinnamon and star anise) and the curry leaves. Stir well, then include the tamarind liquid and simmer for another 5 minutes. Taste gravy for salt and sugar, and adjust to your taste. Garnish and serve.

NESTUM-COVERED CHICKEN WINGS

A favourite when growing up, this recipe has been in my family for over 50 years. It was one of the dishes which my Dutch grandmother often made when all her grandchildren were at home. We used to call it Breakfast Chicken because of the Nestum. Today, I cook this for my twins. As Janice, a very close friend of mine whom I grew up with, and godmother to my children, always emphasizes: "a full kid is a happy kid". This is something that I impart to my little girl and boy as well when I cook for them. They're 4 years old now, and how many kids have a daddy who has cooked all their meals for them since they were infants?

10 chicken wings
2 tablespoons cornflour
1 teaspoon pepper
1 cup seasoned flour (see below)
1 egg, slightly beaten
Nestum, for coating

Marinade
1 tablespoon fresh ginger juice
1 teaspoon light soya sauce
1 teaspoon sesame oil
½ teaspoon palm sugar
   (gula Melaka)
2½ teaspoons five-spice powder

Basic Seasoned Flour
2 cups plain flour
1 tablespoon black pepper
1 teaspoon salt

Variations may include:
1 teaspoon garlic powder
1 teaspoon onion powder
1 teaspoon paprika powder
   (for fish variation)
1 teaspoon ginger powder
   (for fish variation)

Disjoint each wing into two parts and season with cornflour and pepper. Marinate the wings and keep aside for at least 3–5 hours, preferably overnight.

Dredge the wings with the seasoned flour, dip into egg and coat with the Nestum. Deep fry in hot oil until golden.

AJ's Note: To make your own five-spice powder, see page 12.
   Seasoned flour is regular all purpose flour with seasonings added and is easily made. Some people may opt for KFC flour, however I feel its always best to make your own to control what goes into it.
   You can also make Nestum-covered Fish, in which case, season the flour with paprika or ginger.

JA'S SPICED BAKED CHICKEN

This recipe is dedicated to a very special friend of 30 years, Jacinta Felix. She stood by me no matter how much trouble I got myself into in school, she reminded me that in life there is always good in people. Most importantly, she never let me loose my faith and appreciate all that I have to make a better person of myself. Jacinta is truly an angel.

1 chicken, approximately 1.5kg
   (3.3 lbs)
2 tablespoons oil
1 teaspoon salt

Ground together
4 red chillies
1½ teaspoon cumin powder
2 root-ends lemongrass (serai)
3 candlenuts (buah keras)
10 shallots
1 tablespoon coriander powder
½ teaspoon fennel powder
3¾ (1½ in) slice galangal
   (lengkuas)
1¼ cm (½ in) piece turmeric

Ingredients A
2 tablespoons oil
1¾ cup coconut milk
3 teaspoon palm sugar
   (gula Melaka)
1 ping-pong-ball sized tamarind
   paste rendered in ½ cup water

Heat oil and fry the ground ingredients until fragrant. Add 1 teaspoon of salt and remove the mixture from the pan. Rub this mixture all over the chicken, inside the cavity and under the skin of the breasts and thighs also.

Mix ingredients A together in a bowl.

Lay a large sheet of aluminium foil over your roasting dish leaving overhangs on either side that will be used to fold over the chicken. Now place the chicken in the roasting dish and pour the mixture of ingredients A over the chicken.

Preheated an oven to 230°C (450°F). Cook the chicken covered by the foil for 40 minutes. This will ensure that the chicken slow cooks and the juices will be contained within the foil.

After 40 minutes, open the flaps of the foil to expose the chicken to the direct heat of the oven. Roast for another 20 minutes on 230°C (450°F), basting a few times until the chicken is browned and the gravy is thick.

Cut the chicken into serving pieces and pour the remaining gravy over.

B'S CHICKEN CURRY

I made this dish when my wife Barbara was in her first trimester with our twins. She said, "I want to eat chicken curry – something new and fresh, yet spicy and zesty!" You could say I was under a little pressure, but I will do anything for my Boo.

1 chicken, approximately 1.5 kg
　　(3.3 lbs), cut into 12 serving
　　pieces
½ teaspoon salt
1 tablespoon light soya sauce
4 tablespoons oil
2 cups thick coconut milk
2 slices dried 'tamarind' (assam
　　gelugor, assam keping)
Juice from 4 calamansi limes
　　(limau kasturi)
2 kaffir lime (limau perut) leaves
2 tablespoons curry powder
1 tablespoon palm sugar
　　(gula Melaka)
1 cup hot water

Ingredients A
2 kaffir lime (limau perut) leaves
1 large white onion, diced
4 cloves garlic, diced
3 dried chillies, cut into 1 cm
　　(0.4 in) pieces

Ground together
3 big red onions
10-12 dried chillies, soaked in
　　hot water
3 fresh red chillies
2 bird's eye chillies
2½ cm (1 in) shirmp paste
　　(belacan)
5 cm (2 in) ginger
1 slice dried 'tamarind' (assam
　　gelugor, assam keping)

Marinade the chicken with salt and light soya sauce. Pre-heat oil and shallow fry chicken pieces lightly, adding in ingredients A. Allow the chicken to cook and infuse for 8-10 minutes. Remove chicken and set aside.

In the same oil and base ingredients A, fry the ground ingredients until aromatic.

Add the thick coconut milk, 'tamarind' slices, calamansi juice, kaffir leaves, curry powder and palm sugar. Stir in well and put in the chicken with 1 cup of hot water. Cook until the gravy is thick and chicken done.

AJ's Notes: Use 5 bird's eye chillies if you want to feel the burn and call out my name.

HAWAIIAN CHICKEN ROLLS (LEFT)

170 g (6 oz) cooked chicken
   breast, shredded
15 g (½ oz) margarine or butter
15 g (½ oz) flour
4 tablespoons cold milk
200 g (7 oz) canned pineapple,
   drained and finely diced
½ teaspoon salt
½ teaspoon pepper
8 rashers streaky bacon

Melt the margarine over low heat. Remove pan from the heat and stir in the flour, slowly adding the milk to make a roux. Cook slowly until the roux thickens.

Stir in the shredded chicken and drained pineapple. Season with salt and pepper to taste. Allow to cook for 10 minutes.

Divide into eight portions and roll each into a cylinder the size of a cork. Wrap a rasher of bacon around each roll and skewer with a toothpick to hold the bacon.

Preheat an oven to 230°C (450°F). Bake the rolls for about 25 mins until the bacon is crispy.

LEMON CHICKEN WITH MANGO

4 chicken breasts, approximately
   1.5 kg (3.3 lbs)
Oil for deep frying
Strips of ripe mango

Lemon sauce
½ cup lemon juice
2 chicken stock cubes
2 tablespoons cornflour
2½ tablespoons brown sugar
2 tablespoons honey
1 teaspoon grated ginger
1½ cups water

Dipping mixture
½ cup cornflour
3 tablespoons water
4 egg yolks, lightly beaten
¼ teaspoon salt
½ teaspoon pepper

To make the sauce, combine all the sauce ingredients in a saucepan. Cook slowly over medium heat until the sauce thickens.

Mix the cornflour, water, lightly beaten egg yolks, salt and pepper in a bowl. Dip breasts into this mixture and deep fry until golden.

Slice breasts into bite-sized pieces. Spoon over the sauce and garnish with mango strips.

SPICE FRIED CHICKEN

I often get a 'look' or a few knowing smiles when I describe this dish. This is because the recipe includes kas-kas. Kas-kas is basically poppy seeds. Contrary to popular belief, poppy seeds have no narcotic properties because the opium-producing fluid in the bud is only present before the seeds are fully formed. In any case, what's wrong with getting 'high' on a dish?

1 kg (2.2 lbs) chicken parts or drumlettes
1 teaspoon poppy seeds (kas-kas), pounded
Juice from 2 calamansi limes (limau kesturi)
2 cups oil
2 cm (2 in) cinnamon stick
¾ teaspoon salt
1½ tablespoons chilli powder
1 tablespoons turmeric powder (kunyit)
3 root-ends lemongrass (serai)
2 large red onions, finely sliced
2 eggs
½ teaspoon white pepper
Salt to taste

Pounded together
7½ cm (3 in) ginger
15 cloves garlic
1½ teaspoon fennel (jintan manis)

Marinade the chicken in the pounded ingredients, poppy seeds and lime juice for 3 hours.

Heat ¼ cup oil and fry the cinnamon stick. When aromatic, add in the chicken and salt. Cover the pan and cook 5 minutes.

Add in the chilli powder, turmeric powder, lemongrass and onions. Stir occasionally until chicken is done. Remove the chicken and leave to cool. Pour the remaining sauce into a serving dish. (The fried chicken will be placed on this gravy.)

Heat up the remaining 1¾ cups of oil in a clean pan. Beat up 2 eggs with white pepper and salt to taste. Dip the chicken pieces into the egg and deep fry the chicken until crisp. Place the fried chicken pieces on the gravy and serve.

AJ's Note: If poppy seeds are not available, substitute with 1 teaspoon of five-spice powder.

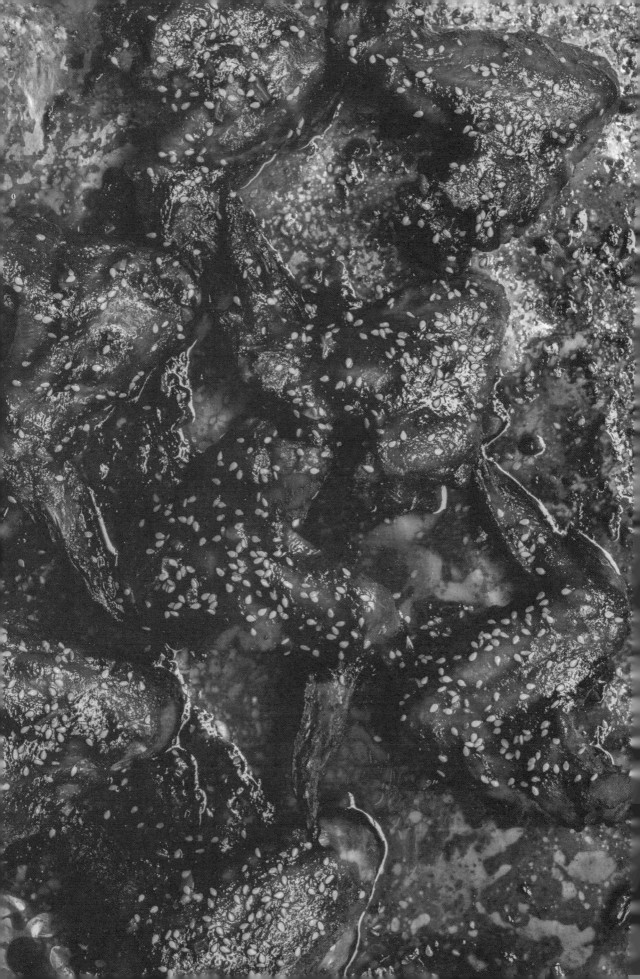

ROASTED CHICKEN WINGS

The preparation of this delicate, tender and juicy dish works in the oven, fried or on a barbecue pit. It is one of those recipes where you dump in the meat into the marinade and let it work its magic.

20 chicken wings, approximately
   1 kg (2.2 lbs)
½ cup sesame seeds

Marinade
3 tablespoons tomato sauce
2 tablespoons brown sugar
2 tablespoons chilli sauce
2 tablespoons sesame oil
1 tablespoons dark soya sauce
1½ tablespoon honey
1½ tablespoon finely diced garlic
1 tablespoon finely diced ginger
1 tablespoon curry powder
½ teaspoon salt

Place the chicken wings into a large mixing bowl. Put all the marinade items into the bowl and massage the mix into the chicken wings. Cover and refrigerate for 4-6 hours.

Once you are ready to oven roast, prepare your tray and layer the bottom with aluminium foil. Preheat the oven to 230°C (450°F), then lower the heat to 180°C (356°F) for cooking.

Place wings on the tray and use the remainder of the marinade for basting. After 15-20 minutes when the underside begins to brown, turn them over and baste the wings again and sprinkle on the sesame seeds.

Return the tray into the oven and cook for a further 20 minutes or to the point where you see the skin getting crisp or the sesame seeds browning.

AJ's Notes: Should you opt to barbecue, cook the underside first, and before you cook the top, mix the sesame seeds with the marinade and brush it on before turning the wings over.

YELLOW CURRY CHICKEN

This is one of the easiest chicken dishes to prepare. Basically everything goes in, and you just need to let it simmer on a low heat. Simple, yet produces an abundance of flavour.

1 chicken, approximately 1.5 kg (3.3 lbs), cut into 12 pieces
4 tablespoons oil
1½ cups thick coconut milk
½ cup warm water
3 potatoes, quartered
2 slices dried 'tamarind' (assam gelugor, assam keping), or use ¼ cup calamansi lime (limau kesturi) juice

Blended together
2 large red onions
2 root-ends lemongrass (serai)
5 candlenuts (buah keras)
1 red chilli
3 cloves garlic
5 cm (2 in) fresh turmeric or 2 level teaspoon turmeric powder
7 green chillies
5 bird's eye chillies (chilli padi)

Pre-heat a pan with the oil. Pour in the blended ingredients and let it simmer on low heat for about 5 minutes. Gently place the chicken pieces into a saucepan, mixing it with the blended ingredients.

Now add in the coconut milk and warm water. Give it a few stirs to mix. Simmer slowly on medium/low heat for about 15 minutes then add in the potatoes and the 'tamarind' slices. Slow cook until the gravy is thick. Add salt and sugar to taste

AJ's Notes: This same curry is good for fish too. Use 1kg (2.2 lbs) garoupa or snapper fillets, cut into 7½ cm (3 in) strips. Once the blended ingredients are simmering, add in the coconut milk and warm water. Put in the fish only then as fish is a soft meat that breaks up easily.

BRIYANI CHICKEN

I decided to deconstruct the Chicken Briyani recipe after a few friends asked if they could just savor the chicken without the briyani rice. I now offer this Briyani Chicken with roti prata or roti chanai (an Indian flat bread similiar to tortilla wraps), or with a salad.

1 chicken, apporximately 1.5 kg
   (3.3 lbs), cut into 8 pieces, or
   6 chicken breasts
20 shallots, finely sliced
1 cup oil

Blended together
12 fresh red chillies
1½ cm (1 in) turmeric

Marinade
2 tablespoons ginger, chopped
2 tablespoons garlic, chopped
½ cup coriander leaves, sliced
½ cup mint leaves, sliced
1 green chilli finely diced
5 cardamoms
4 cloves
5 cm (2 in) cinnamon stick
½ cup yoghurt
1 tablespoon tomato paste

Garnish
¼ cup fried shallots
¼ cup coriander leaves finely
   chopped

Fry the sliced shallots in oil until golden. Remove the fried shallots and set them aside for the marinade and garnishing. Reserve the oil.

Mix 2 tablespoons of the reserved oil, ½ cup fried shallots and the blended paste with all the marinade ingredients. Use this to marinate the chicken for 1 hour.

Heat the balance of the oil from frying the shallots. Slip in the chicken and the marinade and fry to seal the meat. Once all the ingredients are simmering and sticking to the chicken, add ½ cup hot water and slow cook the chicken on medium heat until done. Season with ½ teaspoon of salt or to taste.

Garnish the chicken with the remaining fried shallots and chopped coriander leaves before serving.

AJ's Notes: Do not use the pre-fried shallots that you may obtain from the store for this dish. The key to this dish is the natural onion oil, and for the chicken to absorb the natural flavours of the fried shallots. Pre-fried shallots lack flavour, and the salt added to them will cause the chicken to release fluid, making the chicken dry.

OPOR CHICKEN

This is a classic Indonesian dish, which requires Indonesian laurel (salam leaf) if you are able to obtain it. Odorless when dry, it has a distinct flavour and aroma that is different from bay leaves.

1 chicken or parts, approximately
   5 kg (3.3 lbs)
4 tablespoons oil for frying
2 large white onions, finely
   sliced
½ cup thick coconut milk mixed
   with ½ cup warm water
2 Indonesian laurel leaves
   (salam) or bay leaves
1 root-end lemongrass (serai)
3 strips lemon rind
5 cm (2 in) cinnamon stick
1½ teaspoons grated ginger
1 cup thick coconut milk
1 ping-pong-ball sized tamarind
   paste rendered in ½ cup water
Fried onions

Combined to make a paste
4 cloves garlic, ground
3 candlenuts (buah keras),
   pounded
1 teaspoon pepper
3 teaspoons coriander powder
1 teaspoon cumin powder
   (jintan puteh)
1 teaspoon fennel powder
   (jintan manis)
1 slice galangal (lengkuas),
   ground
½ teaspoon salt
4 tablespoons oil

In a mixing bowl, combine paste and chicken. Rub the paste well into the chicken pieces and keep aside for at least 1 hour.

Heat the oil and fry the sliced onion until golden. Now add the spiced chicken pieces and fry until they just start to colour. Add in the thin coconut milk, Indonesian laurel leaves, lemongrass, lemon rind, cinnamon and grated ginger.

Stir, bring to the boil and cook uncovered for about 20 minutes. The chicken should be done by then.

Add in the thick coconut milk, stir and when about to boil, add in the tamarind liquid. Turn off the heat and check for seasoning. Remove the whole spices and garnish with fried onions.

CARDAMOM CHICKEN

1 chicken, approximately 1.5 kg
   (3.3 lbs), cut into 8 pieces or
   8 chicken thighs
2 tablespoons oil
2 cups coconut milk
4 tablespoons yoghurt
6 green chillies, halved
3 tablespoons chopped coriander
   leaves

Marinade
1 tablespoon grated young
   ginger
2 teaspoons finely chopped
   garlic
3 tablespoons yoghurt
1 teaspoon turmeric powder
1 tablespoon cardamoms, skins
   removed, pounded
2 green chillies, chopped
1 teaspoon cumin powder
   (jintan puteh)
1 teaspoon coriander powder
4 kalamansi lime, juiced and
   rind grated
½ teaspoons salt
½ teaspoons black peppercorns

Blend all the marinade ingredients together and place into a mixing bowl. Toss chicken into the marinade to coat well. Cover and refrigerate overnight.

Heat the oil in saucepan. Remove the chicken from the marinade and fry the chicken until golden. Now add in the balance of the marinade, coconut milk and the 4 tablespoons of yoghurt. Bring to the boil.

Reduce the heat and simmer until chicken is cooked, about 25 minutes. Mix in the fresh coriander and green chillies and serve.

CHICKEN & HAM BITES

I found chicken nuggets boring, so I decided to make these wicked golden gems.

4 chicken thighs, deboned
8 slices ham (3¾ x 7½ cm,
   1½ x 3 in each)
Oil for deep frying

Seasoning
2 teaspoons light soya sauce
2 teaspoons palm sugar
   (gula Melaka)
2 teaspoons Worcestershire
   sauce
1 tablespoon ginger juice
2 teaspoons tapioca flour or
   cornflour
1 teaspoon pepper

Batter
1 egg, lightly beaten
4 tablespoons flour or rice flour
4 tablespoons water

Mix the chicken meat thoroughly with the seasoning. Keep aside for 30 minutes.

Place a thigh flat on a chopping board and put 2 pieces of ham on each chicken thigh. Roll and tie with cooking thread. Place the thighs on a plate and steam for 15 mins. Remove, cut the threads, and cool.

Prepare the batter by mixing the egg into the flour, adding water and beating until smooth.

Cut the chicken into thick slices, dip into batter and fry until golden.

Serve hot or cold on a bed of lettuce.

AJ's Notes: You could also opt to fry these medallions. Sear the rolls on a griddle pan to seal the chicken and the ham so they do not fall apart when you slice them. Dip the chicken and ham coins in the batter and fry till they are golden.

STUFFED CHICKEN WINGS

Whenever I have guests or family over for movie night or a supper treat with wine, stuffed wings always hits the spot. Some time is needed for the preparation, but when you're cooking for friends or family, it is always worth the effort.

10 chicken wings (with no drumlettes)
1 teaspoon turmeric powder (kunyit)
4 tablespoons flour
2 eggs, beaten
Oil for deep frying

Stuffing
1 red chilli, deseeded and chopped
8 shallots, finely chopped
1 spring onion, chopped
2 coriander roots, chopped
150 g (5 oz) minced lean pork
125 g (4 oz) prawns, shelled and chopped
¼ teaspoon salt
½ teaspoon palm sugar (gula Melaka)
1½ teaspoons sesame oil
1½ teaspoons cornflour

The easiest way to debone a wing is to use a pair of kitchen scissiors. Hold the wing tip in one hand and cut off the tips of the bones which joins to the drumlette.

Now all you need to do is push the flesh from the wing tip and draw back the meat and skin to expose both the wing bones, firmly twisting the two bones to dislodge them from the wing tip joint.

Mix together all the stuffing ingredients in a bowl. From the opening of each wing, insert the stuffing into the wings until they are nice and plump. Seal the opening with a bamboo toothpick.

Once all the wings are prepared, sprinkle on the turmeric powder and massage into the wings.

Heat the oil for deep frying. When the oil is hot, dip each stuffed wing with flour, egg and then flour again and deep fry till golden.

Serve the wings with chilli sauce or tomato ketchup.

AJ's Notes: If you have some extra stuffing, it can be rolled into balls, dipped in flour, egg and flour again and deep fried.

SPICED LEMON CHICKEN BALLS

800 g (1.7 lbs) chicken fillet,
   minced
½ teaspoon palm sugar
   (gula Melaka)
1 teaspoon ground black pepper
¼ teaspoon cardamom powder

Spiced yoghurt
2 teaspoons minced ginger
4 red chillies, finely chopped
2 teaspoons coriander powder
1 teaspoon chilli powder
1 teaspoon garam masala
1 teaspoon clarified butter
   (ghee)
1 teaspoon salt
½ cup yoghurt

Sauce
3 tablespoons clarified butter
   (ghee)
2 cups thick coconut milk
½ cup yoghurt
3 teaspoons garam masala
¼ teaspoon cardamom powder
1 tablespoon diced lemon rind
2 teaspoons salt
1 cup water

Put the chicken into the spiced yoghurt. Mix well and shape into ping-pong-ball size.

To make the sauce, heat the 3 tablespoons of ghee in a saucepan, add the coconut milk, yoghurt, garam masala, cardamom powder, lemon rind and salt. Once it begins to boil, add in 1 cup water and bring to a boil again while stirring the sauce.

When boiling, add in the chicken balls. Place them evenly in the pan, using a ladle to scoop the sauce over each meatball. Cover with a lid and cook on medium-low heat, occasionally turning the balls over carefully.

Once the sauce is thick, add in ½ cup of hot water, palm sugar and pepper. Stir again to mix, cover and simmer until dry. Sprinkle the cardamom powder over and serve.

AJ's Notes: The same spiced yoghurt can be used on chicken pieces, drumlettes or chicken thighs that you barbecue. Offer the sauce on the side as a condiment or dip.

THAI CHICKEN FILLETS (LEFT)

Simplicity is the basis of beauty. Anything that is simple as this recipe, yet exquisite in the abundance of flavour, catches our attention. This beautifully seasoned chicken, barbecued over a charcoal fire, is very popular and is sold at roadside food stalls all over Thailand.

500 g (1.1 lb) skinless chicken
    thigh fillets, cut each in half
    and score criss-cross
1 teaspoon turmeric powder
2 teaspoons chilli powder
2 teaspoons chicken stock powder
2 tablespoons oil
2 tablespoon thick coconut milk

Blended together
3 sprigs fresh coriander leaves
4 cloves garlic,
1 tablespoon black peppercorns
4 shallots

Mix all the ingredients together and use it to marinate the chicken. Massage the mix into the chicken fillets as best you can, and set aside to marinate for 2-3 hours.

Grill the chicken pieces 6-7 minutes on each side. Serve with a salad.

CHICKEN IN COCONUT MILK

1 chicken, approximately 1.5 kg
    (3.3 lbs), cut into 12 serving
    pieces, skin removed
½ teaspoon salt
½ teaspoon pepper
½ teaspoon paprika
Oil for deep frying
12 shallots, finely sliced
½ tablespoon chopped garlic
1 tablespoon minced ginger
6 cardamoms
3 star anise
7 cm (2½ in) cinnamon stick
6 cloves
2 cups thick coconut milk
2 teaspoons palm sugar
    (gula Melaka)
1 kaffir lime leaf
1 sprig curry leaves

Season the chicken parts with salt, pepper and paprika powder. Deep fry until golden. Remove and keep aside.

Use 4 tablespoons of the oil in a new pan, and fry the shallots, garlic, ginger and spices until aromatic.

When the shallots, garlic and ginger are golden, add in the coconut milk, palm sugar, kaffir lime leaf and curry leaves. A pinch of salt here to taste is optional.

Bring to a boil and then add in the chicken and slow cook on low heat until the dish is almost dry.

AJ's Note: In some of my chicken dishes, I opt to remove the skin prior to cooking to create a more healthy dish.

IMPERIAL HAWTHORN CHICKEN

If you grew up in Singapoere or Malaysia in the 1950s to the 1980s you'd know haw flakes. They are, in my opinion, a must-have daily snack when growing up. Haw flakes are round candy wafers made from hawthorn berries. I love them, so I decided to cook with them.

4 chicken breasts, halved,
   skinned and deboned
½ teaspoon salt
½ teaspoon sugar
1 tablespoon sesame oil
1 egg white, beaten
2 tablespoons cornflour
1½ cups oil

Sauce
5 cm (2 in) ginger, bruised
10 cloves garlic, bruised
5 rolls haw flakes, crushed
1 tablespoon ketchup
4 tablespoons white vinegar
1½ tablespoons soya sauce
1 teaspoon sugar
1½ teaspoons salt
2 teaspoons cornflour rendered
   in ⅓ cup water
1 teaspoon sesame oil

Chicken
Combine salt, sugar, sesame oil and the beaten egg white and use the mixture to marinate the chicken. Keep aside for 30 minutes before coating the meat thoroughly with the cornflour. Heat the oil and fry 2 pieces of chicken at a time until golden.

Cut the chicken into 5 cm (2 inch) strips and arrange on serving plate.

Sauce
Combine the ginger, garlic, haw flakes, ketchup, vinegar, soya sauce, sugar and salt in ¾ cup warm water and allow to stand for 30 minutes. Strain the mixture into a saucepan and bring to a slow boil. Add the rendered cournflour. Mix well.

Cook over medium heat, stirring until the mixture boils and thickens. Add in the sesame oil and mix well. Pour the sauce over the chicken and serve.

AJ's Note: Known as *shan zha* in Chinese herbal stores, dried hawthorn berries can be obtained as a substiture for haw flakes. Use 2 tablespoons of dried hawthorn berries for of 5 rolls of haw flakes.

MULLIGATAWNY SOUP

Of all the chicken soups made, I would say this is the king of them all although mulligatawny, by name, is pepper water, a combination of Tamil words milagu *(pepper)* thanni *(water). There are many variations of this recipe. When I was in Kochi, I was shown this one, dating back to the 18th century, which uses the ingredients available in the spice country of Kerala.*

1 chicken, approximately 1.5 kg
   (3.3 lbs), cut into 4 pieces
2 star anise
1½ tablespoons oil
10 shallots, sliced
4 cloves garlic, sliced
½ teaspoon fenugreek
2 cups chicken stock
2 cups thick coconut milk mixed
   with 1 cup warm water
1 ping-pong-ball sized tamarind
   paste rendered in ½ cup water
2 stalks curry leaves
¼ teaspoon salt

Ground together
3 tablespooons coriander
1½ tablespoons fennel seeds
6 dried chillies
1⅓ cm (½ in) cinnamon
1 teaspoon mustard seeds
1½ tablespoons cumin
   (jintan putih)
1 teaspoon peppercorns
1⅓ cm (½ in) turmeric (kunyit)
2 cloves

Garnish
12 small shallots, sliced and fried
2 spring onions, chopped
1 bunch coriander leaves, chopped
1 lemon

Boil the chicken and star anise in a medium-sized pot with enough water to cover the chicken. When cooked, remove chicken and shred the meat. Set aside the stock for later use.

Heat the oil in a saucepan and fry the shallots and garlic till golden. Now add in the fenugreek and the ground ingredients. Fry a few minutes till fragrant. Next, add the chicken stock, coconut milk, tamarind liquid, curry leaves and salt. Boil up, then add in the shredded chicken meat.

Serve in a bowl with a little cooked rice or noodles garnished with some fried shallots, spring onions and chopped coriander. Squeeze a little lemon juice over for extra flavour.

MY THAI CHICKEN MASAMAN

1 chicken, approximately 1.5 kg (3.3 lbs), cut into 12 pieces
4 tablespoons oil
1 star anise
2½ cm (1 in) cinnamon stick
3 cloves
2 kaffir lime leaves
1 root-end lemongrass (serai), bruised
1 cup fried coconut
2 tablespoons fish sauce
1½ tablespoon palm sugar (gula Melaka)
4 slices dried 'tamarind' (assam gelugor, assam keping)
1½ cups thick coconut milk
½ teaspoons salt
1½ cups Thai fragrant basil leaves

Blended together
15 dried chillies
10 bird's eye chillies (chilli padi)
7½ cm (3 in) turmeric
2 tablespoons coriander seeds
2 tablespoons black pepper
2 candlenuts (buah keras)
5 cm (2 in) shrimp paste (belacan)
2 kaffir lime leaves
2 root-ends lemongrass (serai)
2 large red onions
5 cm (2 in) galangal (lengkuas)
5 cloves garlic
6 shallots
2½ cm (1 in) ginger

Preheat the oil and lightly fry the blended ingredients for about 10 minutes on medium heat. Once aromatic, add in the whole spices (anise, cinnamon, cloves), kaffir lime leaves and the bruised lemongrass.

Add in chicken and fry and stir to coat the chicken, then add in the fried coconut and continue to simmer for an additional 10 minutes and stir until the oil rises.

Now, add in the fish sauce, palm sugar, 'tamarind' slices, coconut milk and salt. Simmer until fragrant, then add in the basil leaves and cook until the chicken is done.

AJ's Notes: To make fried coconut, fry freshly grated coconut in a non-stick pan without oil until the grated coconut is crisp and slightly brown.

MUTTON & LAMB

MOGLAI CHOPS

I guess something got lost in the translation here, as my grandmother called it "Moglai", but the original name of this old recipe after some research is "Mughlai". Simple to prepare, this is a mouth-watering, palate-dancing and lip-smacking favourite dish for lamb lovers.

6 lamb chops
1 tablespoon ghee (clarified butter)
½ cup warm water
4 medium tomatoes, deseeded and diced
Salt and sugar to taste

Marinade
4 tablespoons yoghurt
1 green chilli, diced
1 sprig coriander leaves, diced
1¼ cm (½ in) ginger, chopped
1 large red onion, finely chopped
3 cloves garlic, chopped
2 heaped teaspoons meat curry powder
1 teaspoon chilli powder
1 teaspoon black pepper
½ teaspoon brown sugar
1 teaspoon salt

Put the chops and the marinade into a large mixing bowl and let the chops soak up the combination of dry and fresh herbs and spices. (Four hours is an adequate marinating time.)

Once ready to cook, pre-heat a heavy saucepan which has a firm-fitting lid. Put in the ghee and place the lamb chops in the pan, searing each side for 4–5 minutes..

Pour in the balance of the marinade, the warm water and the diced tomatoes, mixing them well. Simmer with the pot covered until the chops are cooked and the gravy is almost gone. Check and adjust seasoning of salt or sugar to suit your taste.

LEG OF LAMB IN CITRUS MARINADE

1 leg of lamb
2 tablespoons honey

Marinade
¼ cup brown sugar
Juice from ½ lemon
Juice from 1 orange
3 tablespoons olive oil
3 tablespoons garlic, chopped
2 sprigs rosemary, leaves only
2 teaspoons black pepper
1½ teaspoons salt

Combine all the marinade ingredients in a non stick sauce pan and simmer on low heat until the sugar has melted.

Scald the lamb with hot water and dry with paper towels. Use the end of a paring knife and make 1 cm (0.4 in) X-shaped cuts all over the lamb. Rub the marinade to cover the lamb, pushing bits of garlic, pepper and rosemary into the incisions. Leave to marinate for 2-3 hours.

Place the lamb in a baking dish. Pour some more olive oil over lamb and roast on 162°C (325°F) for 1 hour. Baste occasionally. When done, brush with the honey and let it rest for about 15 minutes before carving.

AJ's Note: Lamb is incomplete without mint sauce or mint pesto. My recipe is below.

MINT SAUCE/PESTO

Juice from 1 lemon
1 tablespoon apple cider vinegar
3 cups mint leaves, finely diced
3 cloves garlic, roughly chopped
½ cup olive oil
½ cup almonds, diced
1 teaspoon sea salt
½ teaspoon black peppercorns, crushed
1 level tablespoon brown sugar

Mix together in a bowl. Ready to serve.

NAVARIN OF LAMB

This stew is a perfect example of what I describe as gentle cooking over a period of time, resulting in full-flavoured meat which falls off the bone or tender melt-in-the-mouth cubes. Navarin is a French ragoût of lamb. The basis of this recipe was first passed to my mother by her sister, my Aunty Mo, some 40 years ago. Aunty Mo, thank you for the recipe and being a part of my cooking journey. As you can see, I have put my own twist on it.

1.2 kg (2½ lb) fillet of lamb, cut into 7½ cm (3 in) cubes
4 tablespoons flour to coat lamb
4 tablespoons butter
5 cloves garlic, crushed
1 large white onion, diced
1 sprig rosemary, leaves only
1 tablespoon flour
2½ cups water
2 beef or chicken stock cubes
300 g (10½ oz) canned tomatoes, chopped
¼ cup tomato puree
350 ml (12 fl oz) white wine
12 shallots sliced
5 strips bacon, chopped
2 tablespoons butter
2 carrots, cut into chunks
2 potatoes, cut into chunks
1 teaspoon brown sugar, optional
2 tablespoons chopped parsley

Toss the lamb cubes in the flour to lightly coat them. Set aside.

Melt 4 tablespoons butter in a pan and sauté the garlic, onion and rosemary leaves. Once lightly browned, add 1 tablespoon of flour. Stir, then add in the water, crumbled stock cubes, canned tomatoes and tomato puree. Stir until smooth. Allow the sauce to boil, then add in wine.

Reduce heat then add in the meat, and simmer covered for 30 minutes.

In a separate pan sauté the shallots and chopped bacon in the 2 tablespoons of butter until the bacon is cooked and slightly crispy.

Pour this mixture into the simmering lamb. Add in the carrots and potatoes. Stir in well and continue to simmer until meat and root vegetables are tender. Check for seasoning, and add a teaspoon of brown sugar if preferred. Put in the chopped parsley just before you serve.

AJ's notes: Personally, I love Viognier, the white wine from the Rhône Valley, for this dish.

A couple of bone-in chops would be perfect additions to this dish. There is a saying: The way into a man's heart is through his stomach. Reflecting on it, I am drawn to Matthew 25:35 – For I was hungry and you gave me food, I was thirsty and you gave me drink, I was a stranger and you welcomed me.

HOT MUTTON OR LAMB CURRY

Both these meats have a strong smell, and people do not often experiment with them in the kitchen. I have found that the addition of some spices and using the right cooking techniques deliver a full-flavoured dish without the odour.

I prefer using Spring lamb with a mix of ribs and legs.

1 kg (2.2 lbs) mutton or lamb,
    cut into serving pieces
5 potatoes, quartered
4 tablespoons oil
½ teaspoon fenugreek (halba)
5 cm (2 in) cinnamon stick
4 cardamoms
4 cloves
2 large red onions, sliced
5 cloves garlic, sliced
5 cm (2 in) fresh ginger, chopped
2 sprigs curry leaves
1 cup thick coconut milk mixed
    with 1½ cups warm water
2 kaffir lime leaves
½ cup thick coconut milk
Juice from 4 calamansi limes
    (limau kesturi)
1 teaspoon poppy seeds
    (kas-kas), pounded
Salt and sugar to taste
1 sprig coriander leaves, chopped

Fried in a dry pan
and ground together
2 tablespoons coriander
2½ teaspoons cumin
20–25 dried chillies, soaked in
    hot water and drained

Boil the quartered potatoes till done, or microwave them in water for 8 minutes.

Fry the fenugreek in the oil lightly until golden to flavour the oil. Remove and discard the fenugreek. In the flavoured oil, fry the cinnamon, cardamom and cloves, then add in the onions, garlic, ginger and curry leaves and continue frying until they become soft.

Add in the ground ingredients, frying until aromatic and the oil rises. Then put in the mutton, mix awhile, then include the diluted coconut milk and kaffir lime leaves. Cook for about 25 minutes on low heat.

Now add in the thick coconut milk, cooked potatoes, calamansi juice and poppy seeds. Stir and cook until the potatoes and meat are done. Season with salt and some sugar and then turn the flame low and slow cook till gravy thickens. Dish out and garnish with coriander leaves.

AJ's Note: Use more or less dried chillies depending on how much heat you wish the dish to have.

DRY MEAT CURRY

This recipe can be used for pork, beef, mutton, chicken and venison.

450 g (1 lb) middle neck of
   lamb, cut into 5 cm (2 in)
   cubes
1 tablespoon turmeric (kunyit)
   powder
1½ teaspoons rice vinegar
3 tablespoons oil
2 large red onions, diced
4 cloves
4 cardamoms
1½ cm (1 in) cinnamon stick
½ cup water
1½ tablespoons chilli powder or
   freshly ground chilli paste
2 potatoes, cubed
1 sprig curry leaf
½ teaspoon palm sugar
   (gula Melaka)
½ cup coconut milk
1 tablespoon fennel seeds, dry
   fried and pounded

Pounded together
2½ cm (1 in) ginger
2 cloves garlic

Marinate the cubed meat with the turmeric, vinegar and the pounded ginger and garlic. Set aside.

Pre-heat the oil, then fry the sliced onions with the cloves, cardamoms and cinnamon stick. Once the onions are glazed, add in the marinated meat and fry until the liquid dries up.

Now add in the water, chilli powder, potatoes, curry leaves and palm sugar. Reduce heat and cooking on a low simmer until liquid dries up. Once dried, add in the coconut milk and stir. Finally, put in the pounded fennel seed. Stir and simmer until the consistency is thick.

LAMB KOORMA

1 kg (2.2 lbs) lamb, cut into
    bite-sized pieces
1 cup yoghurt
1 teaspoon salt
6 tablespoons oil
2 medium-sized potatoes, cubed
¾ cup large red onion, chopped
2 cups hot water
1 cup thick coconut milk
¾ tablespoon palm sugar
    (gula Melaka)
1 tablespoon white pepper
½ cup cashew nuts
¼ cup chopped coriander leaf
Juice of 1 calamansi lime

Spices & Herbs
3 cardamoms
4 cloves
2 star anise
2 pandan leaves
4 cm (1½ in) cinnamon stick

Blended together
10 cloves garlic
7½ cm (3 in) ginger
2 tablespoons coriander
2 tablespoons cumin
    (jintan putih)
2 tablespoon fennel
    (jintan manis)
2 dried red chillies, soaked in
    hot water

Place the lamb in a mixing bowl with the yoghurt and salt. Mix well and allow to marinate for 2 hours.

Heat the oil and on low heat and fry the spices and herbs and the potatoes until aromatic. Once the potatoes are browning, remove and set them aside. Now add in the onions and fry until glassy.

Add in the blended ingredients, and fry till aromatic. Then add in the lamb and mix well until the meat is well coated. Allow to sear for about 5 minutes.

Now add in the hot water, coconut milk, palm sugar and place the lid on the pan to simmer on low for about 45 minutes, periodically stirring to ensure that the meat does not stick to the bottom of the pan. During this time, the texture will reduce to a thick, wet consistency.

Now add in the white pepper, potatoes and cashew nuts. Stir in well and the dish is ready to be served. Garnish with some coriander leaves and calamansi juice.

AJ's Notes: This same method can be used for beef, chicken, and mutton.
   Increase the amount of dried red chillies in the blended ingredients to feel more love!

BLACK PEPPER LAMB CHOPS

This recipe can also be used for beef ribs, mutton and venison with bone on.

1 kg (2.2 lbs) lamb chops
4 tablespoons ghee (clarified
 butter)
1 cup yoghurt
1 teaspoon palm sugar
 (gula Melaka)
2 teaspoon dark soya sauce

Ingredients A
2 tablespoons black peppercorns,
 dry roasted and coarsely
 pounded
1 tablespoon cumin powder
8 cloves
10 cloves garlic, pounded
7½ cm (3 in) ginger, pounded

Ingredients B
4 cm (1½ in) cinnamon stick
3 large red onions
2 sprigs curry leaves
1 teaspoon mixed spices for fish
 curry

Mix lamb chops with ingredients A and allow to marinate for about 1 hour.

Put the lamb chops into a saucepan with 3 cups water and bring to the boil. Lower heat and simmer until the mutton is tender and getting dry. If the water dries up and the meat is still not tender, pour in another cup of water and continue to simmer.

In a separate pan, melt the ghee and sauté ingredients B until fragrant. Add to mutton and then include the yoghurt, palm sugar and dark soya sauce. Mix well.

Continue frying until the lamb chops are well coated with the gravy and spices and is dry. Serve with rice or naan bread.

AJ's Note: You did not read it wrong; this meat dish uses mixed spices for fish curry.

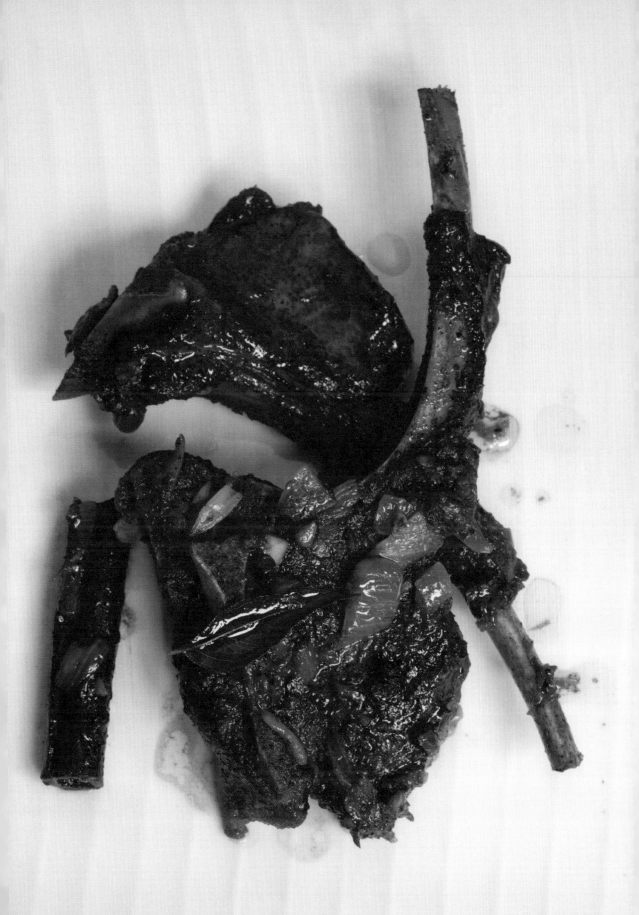

MADRAS MUTTON

This recipe is only completely well-prepared if you have sweat trickling down your forehead and neck as you eat the dish, and every firey mouthful is followed by a murmur of deep satisfaction.

1 kg (2.2 lbs) mutton, cut into bite-sized (5 cm, 2 in) pieces
2 cups coconut milk
2 cups hot water
5 cm (2 in) cinnamon stick
2 teaspoons turmeric (kunyit) powder
30 g (1 oz) tamarind paste, mixed with ¾ cup water
1 teaspoon palm sugar
2 sprigs curry leaves
4 tablespoons oil

Ground together
15 dried red chillies, pre-soaked in hot water
4 fresh red chillies
4 bird's eye chillies (chilli padi)
1 teaspoon cumin (jintan putih), toasted
1 teaspoon fennel (jintan manis), toasted
½ tablespoon palm sugar
10 shallots
6 cloves garlic
2 slices fresh ginger
Salt to taste

Side Salad
1 cucumber, deseeded and diced
1 cup chopped parsley
1 cup chopped canned pineapple
4 tablespoons yoghurt
1 calamansi lime, juiced
¼ teaspoon cinnamon powder

Mix the coconut milk and hot water in a pan and bring it to a boil. Add in the cinnamon, turmeric, tamarind liquid, palm sugar and curry leaves. Turn the heat to low. and cook for about 2-3 minutes before including the mutton. Allow to simmer for 20 minutes.

In a separate pan, heat up the oil, and fry the ground ingredients for a few minutes until aromatic. Once the mutton has simmered for 20 minutes, add in the fried aromatic ingredients and stir in well. Allow to simmer until gravy thickens and meat is well coated.

Mix all the ingredients for the side salad and serve with the curry.

RAGOUT OF LAMB

1 kg (2.2 lbs) lamb shoulder, cut into bite-sized (7½ cm, 3 in) pieces or diced if you want to serve it over pasta
2 teaspoons fresh ginger juice
¼ teaspoon nutmeg powder
½ teaspoon fresh ground black peppercorns
3 tablespoons seasoned flour
4 tablespoons olive oil
6 cloves garlic, minced
1 star anise
4 cm (1½ in) cinnamon stick
1 large white onion, diced
2½ cups chicken stock
300 g (10.5 oz) canned chopped tomatoes
¼ cup tomato puree
¼ cup chopped flat leaf parsley
1 teaspoon lemon rind, finely diced
Salt to taste

For pasta (optional)
1 cup red wine
2 cups chicken stock
3 tablespoons green peas
Grated cheese

Place the lamb in a mixing bowl. Add in the ginger juice, nutmeg powder and ground peppercorns. Mix it in well until the meat is coated with the spices. Add the flour to seal the spices. Set aside, and allow to marinade for about 2 hours or overnight if you prefer.

Heat the oil in a pan, and lightly sear the lamb until its golden brown on each side. Now add in the minced garlic, star anise, cinnamon stick, onion and cook, while stirring, until the garlic is slightly brown.

Include the chicken stock, tomatoes, and tomato puree. Allow to simmer on low heat for about 30 minutes, stirring occasionally. You should have a thick consistency. Once the meat is tender, stir in the parsley and lemon rind. Ready to serve.

AJ's Notes: You can make fresh ginger juice by blending ginger and extracting the juice.
This recipe is great served on top of mashed potatoes.

For Pasta: Ensure that the lamb is diced when you cook this recipe to be served with buttered pasta. Note the reduced amount of chicken stock, when you include the red wine. Green peas are added at the same time you add in the parsley and lemon rind. Top with grated cheese.

ROGAN JOSH

This is a classic Persian dish, although Rogan is a very distinguished and long-established surname of early medieval Irish origin. It means: compassionate, methodical, believe in law, tolerant and like to help humanity.

1 leg of lamb, bone in, cut by
    your butcher into 8¾ cm
    (3.5 in) pieces
2 tablespoons clarified butter
    (ghee)
2 cardamoms
2 bay leaves
2 cloves
6 whole black peppercorns
1 star anise
4 cm (1½ in) cinnamon stick
12 shallots, sliced
½ teaspoon turmeric powder
1½ teaspoons chilli powder
4 teaspoons paprika
1 teaspoon cumin (jintan putih),
    ground
2 sprigs fresh coriander, with
    roots, chopped
6 tablespoons yoghurt
1 cup tomatoes, deseeded and
    diced
1 cup hot water
½ teaspoon salt
½ teaspoon sugar

Garnish
Chopped corinader leaves

AJ's special paste
10 cloves garlic
7½ cm (3 in) ginger
2 blades of mace or 1 flat
    teaspoon nutmeg powder
2 cloves
12 whole black peppercorns
2 cardamoms
12 unsalted almonds
4 teaspoons paprika
¾ cup water

Heat the ghee until it liquefies, and fry the cardamoms, bay leaves, cloves, peppercons, star anise and cinnamon in the hot ghee. Stir and wait until the cloves swell and the bay leaves begin to take on colour. Now add in the sliced shallots and lightly fry till light brown, then add in the special paste and simmer until aromatic.

Put in the lamb, turmeric, chilli powder, paprika, cumin and coriander. Stir and coat lamb well. Once this is done, add in yoghurt and tomatoes. Mix it all in well, ensuring you scrape all the spices from the bottom of the pot,

Add the 1 cup (250ml) hot water. Bring to the boil, cover and cook on low for 45 minutes (or until meat is tender.) Include ½ teaspoon each of salt and sugar, or to taste at the end. Garnish with chopped coriander leaves.

AJ's Notes: The lacy aril from the outer shell of the nutmeg, once dried, becomes yellowish-brown mace. Mace is sold in whole pieces called blades or in the more commonly-found ground form.

If you prefer chicken, use the recipe with 1.5 kg (3.3 lbs) chicken, with or without the skin.

If you prefer beef, I recommend a mixture of lean beef and short ribs.

GULAI KAMBING (MUTTON CURRY)

The term "gulai" is commonly used for the rich and spicy infused curries from Malaysia and Indonesia. The remarkable thing about this dish is when food lovers describe it, it is often with facial and hand gestures to describe its intense flavours.

1 kg (2.2 lbs) mutton, cut into
   bite-sized (5 cm, 2 in) pieces
30 g (1 oz) tamarind paste,
   mixed with ¾ cup water
1½ teaspoon chilli powder
½ teaspoon cinnamon powder
½ teaspoon nutmeg powder
4 tablespoons olive oil
4 cloves
2 cups coconut milk
1 root-end lemongrass (serai)
   crushed
5 slices ginger
6 slices galangal (lengkuas)
1 turmeric (kunyit) leaf,
   shredded
2 kaffir lime leaf
½ cup chopped coriander leaves
Juice from 4 calamansi limes

Ground together
15 black peppercorns
1 stalk lemongrass (serai) root
4 slices fresh turmeric (kunyit)
10 shallots
4 cloves garlic
1 tablespoon coriander seeds,
   toasted
½ teaspoon cumin (jintan putih),
   toasted
1 tablespoon palm sugar

Place the mutton into a mixing bowl and add in the tamarind liquid, and chilli, cinnamon and nutmeg powders. Mix in well and allow to marinade for 3 hours. Note that mutton smells gamey and the longer you marinade it, the better it would be.

Heat up the oil in a pan, and fry the ground ingredients and cloves for a few minutes until aromatic, then add in the marinated meat and all the marinade in the mixing bowl.

When simmering, pour in coconut milk, lemongrass, ginger, galangal, and the turmeric and kaffir lime leaves, allowing the ingredients to mix into the meat well.

Simmer on a low heat for 25 minutes, stirring occasionally. Once ready, stir in the coriander leaves and calamansi juice and serve.

PORK

GOLDEN CRISP PORK BELLY VINDALOO

This dish is derived from the Portuguese Carne de Vinha D'alhos, a pork dish native to Madeira that is infused with wine and garlic. The Goanese substituted the wine with vinegar and added the fresh chillies and additional spices to evolve this dish into Vindaloo.

1 kg (2.2 lbs) pork belly, cut into 2½ cm (1 inch) slices
2 tablespoons white rice vinegar
½ teaspoon salt
3 tablespoons oil
1 teaspoon brown sugar
1 tablespoon of black vinegar

Ground together
2 teaspoons turmeric (kunyit) powder
3 tablespoons coriander
3 tablespoons cumin (jintan putih)
5 cm (2 in) ginger
3 whole pods garlic, about 15 cloves garlic
10 fresh reds chillies
6 dried chillies
½ teaspoon black pepper
½ teaspoon mustard seeds

Place the pork into a mixing bowl. Rub in the ground ingredients together with the vinegar and salt into the pork. Allow to sit for an hour.

Pre-heat the oil in a pan and, when hot, fry the pork on medium heat, turning well. As the belly pork is naturally fatty, the idea is to get the belly fat golden and a little crispy.

Once you have obtained the required texture of the pork, switch off the fire, put in the brown sugar and black vinegar and give it a quick stir and serve.

A SIMPLE PORK CURRY

As the name states, this recipe is simple. Yet it is full of flavour. It is a great dish to prepare for the family on weekends. Served with coconut rice, it transforms the dish from 'simple' to 'to die for'.

½ kg (1.1 lbs) pork belly, cut into 2½ cm (1 inch) cubes or sliced

¼ kg (0.55 lbs) lean pork, cut into 2½ cm (1 in) cubes or sliced

6 tablespoons oil

½ cup coconut cream

1 tablespoon palm sugar (gula Melaka)

Salt to taste

Blended together

2 tomatoes, deseeded

1½ tablespoons tomato paste

15 dried chillies

5 cm (2 in) ginger, chopped

1 teaspoon fennel seeds, dry roasted (see notes)

1 teaspoon cumin seeds, dry roasted (see notes)

2 large red onions

10 cloves garlic

Pre-heat the oil and fry the blended ingredients until fragrant and aromatic. Add in the pork, and continue to fry for 8 minutes until the pork is coated. Now flatten out the pork to cover the surface of the pan, then add enough hot water to cover pork.

Cook over a low simmering heat, stirring from time to time, until the pork is done. Add in the coconut cream, palm sugar, and the salt to taste.

AJ's Notes: Dry roasting any spice is a simple procedure, yet very important to ensure the aroma and flavour of the spice is fully extracted. A non-stick pan is all that is required. Pre-heat the pan without oil and place the spice in and gently turn it to the point when you can get the scent of the spice.

Coconut Rice is very easy to prepare in your rice cooker. Once the rice is washed, and the required amount of water you would use in standard rice cooking is place in, just add in ¼ cup of thick coconut milk for every 2 cups of rice and stir in. In addition you could also drop in a kaffir lime leaf or a pandanus leaf.

SWEET AND SOUR PORK

Whenever I make this dish, I can't help but think of the older Chinese-American kung-fu movies. My version of the master says: "The secret of perfect balance of sweet and sour taste lies in the soul of the ingredients used."

½ kg (1.1 lbs) pork, cut into
   2½ cm (1 inch) cubes
1 teaspoon five-spice powder
1 teaspoon soya sauce
1 cup flour for coating meat
2 egg yolks, beaten
Oil for deep frying
1 large white onion, quartered
½ red or yellow capsicum, cut
   into chunks
10 pineapple cubes from a can
1 tomato, quartered
¼ cucumber, deseeded and cut
   into chunks

Sauce
3 tablespoons cornflour
½ cup pineapple juice from
   canned pineapples cubes
¼ cup sugar
3 tablespoons soya sauce
½ cup vinegar
3 tablespoons Chinese Shaoxing
   rice wine or brandy
3 tablespoons tomato sauce
1 tablespoon plum sauce

To make the sauce base, first mix the cornflour in the pineapple juice. Next, combine the sugar, soya sauce, vinegar, rice wine, tomato sauce and plum sauce in a saucepan and bring to a boil. Add the cornflour and pineapple juice mixture slowly. Cook for about a minute and set aside.

Now, season the pork with five-spice powder and soya sauce. Roll the seasoned pork in the flour, dip in the beaten egg yolk, then roll in the flour again. Set the prepared pork aside.

Pre-heat the oil. Dip the pork in the beaten egg yolk again before deep frying. Place the fired pork in a serving dish.

Put 3 tablespoons of the oil from the deep frying into a fresh pan. Brown the onions lightly then add in the capsicum and the sauce. Cook for about 1 minute, then include the pineapple cubes, tomato and cucumber, and bring to a boil. Pour over the pork and serve.

AJ's Note: You may also marinade your pork in five-spice powder and soya sauce and refrigerate it for a few hours prior to coating it with flour and beaten egg yolk.

DEEP FRIED PORK WITH SPICY SESAME SAUCE

300 g (10.5 oz) belly pork cut
    into 2½ cm (1 in) cubes
Oil for deep frying
Sesame seeds, toasted
1 chilli, chopped

Marinade
¼ teaspoon five-spice powder
½ teaspoon black soya sauce
½ teaspoon pepper
1 teaspoon sugar
1 egg
1 tablespoon flour
1 teaspoon cornflour

Sauce
¼ cup water
½ teaspoon black soya sauce
1 tablespoon honey
3 tablespoons tomato sauce
1 teaspoon sugar
1 teaspoon sesame oil
3 bird's eye chillies (chilli padi),
    diced
1 tablespoon sesame seeds,
    toasted

Marinate the pork with the marinade for 4–5 hours, preferably overnight in the refrigerator.

Once ready, pre-heat the oil and deep fry the pork over medium heat until the meat is cooked, golden and crispy.

Combine all the sauce ingredients, except the sesame seeds, in a separate pan and simmer gently until the sauce is syrupy and thick. Once this consistency is achieved add the sesame seeds and stir.

Put the pork in the sauce and give it a good stir before dishing out.

Sprinkle with sesame seeds and the chopped chilli before serving.

AJ's Notes: Bird's eye chillies can vary in the level of heat. Vary the number of chillies to your level of spice tolerance: 1-2 (light spicy), 3-4 (your forehead begins to sweat), 5-6 (a tingling sensation on your scalp and palate with sweat running down your cheeks), 8-10 (you're in for a ride).

PORK RIB VINDALOO

There's just something about ribs that awaken the caveman in us all. It's my type of comfort food.

1 kg (2.2 lbs) large pork ribs,
    each rib cut into two
3 tablespoons oil
5 cloves garlic, pounded
2 large red onions, sliced
¼ teaspoon coriander powder
2 teaspoons mustard seeds,
    coarsely pounded
½ cup white vinegar
Sugar and salt to taste

Ground together
1½ tablespoons cumin seeds
25 dried chillies
2½ cm (1 inch) turmeric
5 cm (2 in) ginger

Pre-heat the oil and fry the garlic until it is soft, then add in the sliced onions and fry for awhile until they become glassy.

Now pour in the ground ingredients and simmer. Once aromatic, add in the pork ribs, coriander powder, mustard seeds and vinegar. Simmer for a further 10 minutes, then add in a little water to just about cover the meat. Cook slowly over low simmer for 15 minutes.

When the pork is almost cooked, add in some sugar and salt to taste. This is a dryish dish.

AJ's Note: If you love to experiment, this dish can also be done with chicken drumlettes.

CHINESE ROAST PORK RIBS

You may also opt to use this recipe for barbequeing, or grilling the ribs depending on your preference of cooking style and dining experience.

1 kg (2.2 lbs) pork ribs, cut each
    into thirds

Seasoning
3 cloves garlic, minced
1 teaspoon five-spice powder
2 teaspoons bicarbonate of soda
1 tablespoon chilli sauce
2 tablespoons hoi sin sauce
1 tablespoon black soya sauce
2 tablespoons light soya sauce
2 tablespoons Chinese rice wine
1½ teaspoon salt
3 tablespoons palm sugar
    (gula Melaka) or brown sugar
1 teaspoon pepper
3 tablespoons water

Mix the seasoning ingredients in a bowl and use it to rub all over the pork. Let it marinate overnight in the refrigerator.

The next day, brush the meat with oil and roast for 45 minutes in a 175°C (350°F) oven until done.

COFFEE PORK RIBS

This ribs dish has a few "secret" ingredients in the marinade and a rich sauce that makes it special.

1 kg (2.2 lbs) baby back ribs,
  cut each into two
2 egg whites
1 cup flour, for coating
Oil for deep frying
2 tablespoons oyster sauce
2 tablespoon Worcestershire
  sauce
1 teaspoon dark soya sauce
½ teaspoon sesame oil
3 teaspoons cornflour, mixed in
  1 cup water

Marinade
3 tablespoons olive oil
2 tablespoons oyster sauce
2 teaspoons bicarbonate of soda
1 tablespoon sesame oil
½ teaspoon brown sugar
¼ teaspoon cinnamon powder
¼ teaspoon five-spice powder
2 teaspoons flour
2 teaspoons potato flour

Sauce
½ cup water
1 teaspoon brown sugar
1 teaspoon cocoa powder
1¼ tablespoons unsweetened
  coffee powder
2 teaspoons maltose syrup

Place all the ribs in a mixing bowl, pour in the marinade and rub it all over the pork. Let it marinate overnight in the refrigerator. Before you deep fry the ribs, dip it in egg whites then into the flour for coating. Deep fry all the ribs and set aside.

To prepare the sauce, first bring the water to a slow simmer, and add in the brown sugar, cocoa powder, coffee powder and maltose syrup. Once mixed, add in the oyster sauce, Worcestershire sauce, dark soya sauce and sesame oil. You will now have a soupy consistency.

Slowly add in the cornflour mixture, stirring to get a thick and sticky sauce. Once you have required the desired consistency, pour in the ribs, toss and serve.

AJ's Note: Hershey's cocoa powder is good for this dish.

CHINESE HONEY ROAST PORK RIBS

1 kg (2.2 lbs) pork ribs, cut each
    into thirds

Marinade
3 tablespoons honey
3 cloves garlic, pureed
½ teaspoon five-spice powder
2 teaspoons bicarbonate of soda
2 tablespoons oyster sauce
1 tablespoon black soya sauce
2 tablespoons light soya sauce
1 flat teaspoon garlic powder
½ teaspoon salt
½ teaspoon pepper

Coating
2 tablespoons oil
2 tablespoons water
1 tablespoon honey

Mix the marinade ingredients in a bowl and use it to rub all over the pork ribs. Let it marinate overnight in the refrigerator.

The next day, brush the meat with coating sauce and roast for 45 minutes in a 175°C (350°F) oven until done.

AJ's Notes: You may also opt to barbeque, or grill the ribs. With honey as a base, always remember not to expose the ribs too long to an open flame, as this will result in the meat burning on the outside, but remaining uncooked on the inside. Cooking over embers on a barbeque is always best for ribs.

SIZZLING PORK RIBS

1 kg (2.2 lbs) baby back ribs, cut
    each into thirds
½ orange

Marinade
4 cloves garlic, ground
6 bird's eye chillies, finely diced
5 cm (2 in) young ginger, ground
6 tablespoons honey mustard
½ cup marmalade
2 tablespoons dark soya sauce
2 tablespoons Worcestershire
    sauce
2 tablespoons palm sugar
    (gula Melaka)
1½ teaspoon onion salt
1 teaspoon ground black
    peppercorns

Place all the ribs in a mixing bowl, pour in the marinade and rub it all over the pork. Let it marinate overnight in the refrigerator.

This recipe works exceptionally well on the BBQ pit. A slow cook over charcoal ember is the perfect cooking style. Once the ribs are cooked, squeeze over the juice from the orange and serve.

Should you prefer to use the oven, brush the marinated meat with some olive oil and roast for 45 minutes in a 175°C (350°F) oven until done.

PORK LEMONGRASS CURRY

500 g (1.1 lbs) pork, cut into
   2½ cm (1 in) cubes
6 tablespoons of oil
2 large potatoes, quartered,
   optional
1 cup milk
½ teaspoon palm sugar
   (gula Melaka)
Juice from 4 calamansi limes
   (limau kesturi) or 2 tablespoons
   vinegar
Sugar to taste

Blended together
2 large red onions
2 root-ends lemongrass (serai)
4 cloves garlic
4 candlenuts (buah keras)
1¼ cm (½ in) shrimp paste
   (belacan), cut width-wise from
   a 10 x 5 x 5 cm (5 x 2 x 2 in)
   block, toasted
2½ cm (1 in) ginger
15 dried chillies
3 red chillies
1 teaspoon mustard
1 teaspoon turmeric powder
1 stalk curry leaves

Pre-heat the oil and fry the blended ingredients until aromatic. Put in the pork and mix well. Fry for about 8-10 minutes until the pork turns white and is coated well. It is normal for the pork to give out a little water. Continue to simmer on a low heat.

If using potatoes, place them in a bowl with enough water to cover them. Cook them in a microwave for 12 minutes on high. This would three-quarter cook them.

Pour in enough water to cover the simmering pork. Cook over low heat until the meat is soft, then add in the milk, palm sugar and pre-cooked potatoes. Allow to simmer for a further 15 minutes. Stir and add the lime and sugar, both to taste.

AJ's Note: Chicken Lemongrass Curry can also be prepared the same way, with the same amount of chicken, but using 1 cup of thick coconut milk instead of regular milk.

SLICED PORK IN TOMATO SAUCE

½ kg (1.1 lbs) loin pork, sliced
4 tablespoons oil
Sesame seeds, optional

Marinade
2 tablespoons palm sugar
  (gula Melaka)
½ teaspoon five-spice powder
2 tablespoons tapioca flour
1 teaspoon bicarbonate of soda
1 tablespoon Chinese Shaoxing
  rice wine
1 tablespoon dark soya sauce

Sauce
4 shallots, sliced thinly
1 red chilli, sliced thinly
4 tablespoons tomato ketchup
2 tablespoons Lingams chilli
  sauce
1 teaspoon palm sugar
  (gula Melaka) or brown sugar
2 tablespoon light soya sauce
3 tablespoons water

Pound the pork lightly with a mallet to tenderise and mix together with the marinade. Let it marinate for at least 1 hour or overnight.

Heat the cooking oil in a pan and fry the slices of pork on both sides until slightly brown. Remove and keep aside.

To prepare the sauce, heat the remaining cooking oil and fry the shallots until they become soft. Add in the rest of the sauce ingredients and bring to a boil. Return the pork to sauce and stir until evenly coated. Garnish with some sesame seeds if you wish.

AJ's Notes: Fry the pork slices to your preferred consistency. Some people may like to have the pork a little more crispy. In that case, all you need to do is to fry it a little longer.

DEVIL CURRY

Made by the devil in me….

½ kg (1.1 lbs) pork belly, cut
    into 2½cm (1 inch) cubes
2 tablespoons butter
1 small can cubed pineapple,
    approximately 230 g
2 tablespoons oil
1 cup coconut cream
2 tablespoons vinegar
2 tablespoons chilli sauce
2 cups hot water
2 small potatoes, cubed
1 carrot, cubed
Sugar and salt to taste

Ground together
10 dried chillies
8 shallots
4 bird's eye chillies (chilli padi)
4 cloves garlic
2 root-ends lemongrass (serai)
½ teaspoons turmeric powder
3 candlenuts (buah keras)
1 sprig curry leaves
3 cloves garlic
2½ cm (1 in) young ginger
5cm (2 in) galangal (lengkuas)
1 teaspoon mustard seeds

Fry the pork belly to your preferred consistency in the butter. If you like to have the pork a little more crispy, all you need to do is fry it a little longer. Set aside. Discard the syrup from the pineapples and fry the pineapples as well. Set aside.

Add the oil to the remaining butter and fry the ground ingredients until fragrant. Slowly stir in the coconut cream, vinegar and chilli sauce and bring it to a boil. Now add in the pork and 2 cups of hot water, followed by the potatoes and carrots.

Cook for another 15 minutes on a low simmer until the gravy thickens. Add the fried pineapple and sugar and salt to taste. Serve.

ROASTED AND SWEET PORK DEVIL CURRY (RIGHT)

This is a spiced-up combination of roasted pork (siu yuk) and sweet pork (char siu).

½ kg (1.1 lbs) mixed roast pork
  and sweet pork, sliced
4 tablespoons oil
2 small potatoes, cubed
1 carrot, cubed
1 teaspoon mustard seeds,
  pounded slightly
2 tablespoons vinegar
1 cup coconut cream
Sugar and salt to taste
2 tablespoons chilli sauce

Ground together
10 dried chillies
2 fresh red chillies
2 root-ends lemongrass (serai)
½ teaspoon turmeric powder
3 candlenuts (buah keras)
1 sprig curry leaves
3 cloves garlic
2½ cm (1 in) ginger

Fry the ground ingredients in the oil until fragrant. Pour in 2 cupfuls of hot water and bring to a boil.

Add the potatoes and carrots and cook about 10 minutes, then add in all the pork and mustard seeds.

Cook for another 10 minutes then include the vinegar, the coconut cream, salt and sugar to taste. The gravy should be thick at this time. Finally, add in the chilli sauce.

AJ's Note: This dish can be made with any leftover roasted meats, beef, chicken, sausages and even luncheon meat

FRIED PORK BALLS

½ kg (1.1 lbs) minced pork
Oil for deep frying
Flour for coating
Coriander leaves

Marinade
3 sprigs coriander with roots,
  finely diced
2 teaspoons black peppercorns
  crushed
4 cloves garlic, finely diced
4 shitake mushrooms, finely
  diced
1 red chilli, deseeded and finely
  diced
2 tablespoons fish sauce
1 teaspoon brown sugar

Place the minced pork in a mixing bowl. Add in the marinade and massage the ingredients into the pork. Although the meat is minced, pounding the meat with your fist or palms, like kneading bread, softens the pork to an even smoother paste.

Once the pork is mixed, proceed to make balls of 2½ cm (1 in) in size, rolling them in both palms.

Heat the oil for deep frying. Coat the balls with flour and deep fry a few at a time until they are golden.

Place the fried pork balls in a dish and garnish with the coriander leaves. Serve hot with chilli and garlic sauce.

SRI LANKAN FRIED PORK CURRY

1 kg (2.2 lbs) belly pork,
  skinned and cut into 5cm
  (2 inch) cubes
3 tablespoons oil
2 stalks curry leaves
¼ teaspoon fenugreek (halba)
2 medium-sized red onions,
  finely chopped
4 cloves garlic, chopped
5 cm (2 in) ginger, finely
  chopped
3 tablespoons curry powder
2 teaspoons chilli powder
2 teaspoons salt
1 tablespoon vinegar
1 tablespoon tamarind pulp
  rendered in 1½ cups hot water
5 cm (2 in) cinnamon
4 cardamoms
1 cup thick coconut milk or
  3 tablespoons yoghurt
1 tablespoon clarified butter
  (ghee)
Sugar to taste

Heat the oil and fry the curry leaves and fenugreek until they start to brown. Add in the onion and garlic and fry until soft.

Now add in the ginger, curry powder, chilli powder, salt, pork and vinegar. Fry nicely until well mixed.

Now include the tamarind liquid plus the cinnamon and cardamoms in the pan. Mix well. Cover and cook on low heat until the meat is tender, about 1 hour.

If using milk, add now or put in the yoghurt a spoon at a time into the meat. Mix well.

Remove the meat and fry in another pan with 1 tablespoon of clarified butter until the meat is nicely browned. Return the meat to the gravy, add a little sugar to taste and mix well. Ready to serve.

SPICY PORK TROTTERS

1 pork trotter, cut into 8-10
   serving pieces
8 tablespoons oil
6 cloves garlic, bruised with skin on
6 pieces old ginger, each 5cm
   (2 in), bruised
4 dried red chillies, each cut into
   thirds
1 stick cinnamon, approximately
   5 cm (2 in)
6 tablespoons dark soya sauce
4 tablespoons black rice vinegar
2 tablespoons palm sugar
   (gula Melaka)

Blended
6 fresh red chillies
8 dried red chillies
1 tablespoon preserved soya beans
   (taucheong)
5 cm (2 in) ginger
6 cloves garlic

Heat the oil and fry the blended ingredients until aromatic. Now add in the pork and fry for at least 10 minutes, searing the pork to seal the meat and infuse the blend into the meat.

Now add in all the remaining ingredients, stir and continue to simmer for a further 10 minutes. Transfer to a pressure cooker.

Pour in enough hot water to just about cover the meat. Pressure cook for about 15 minutes till tender.

AJ's Notes: Should a pressure cooker not be available to you, you can use a regular pot to cook the trotters, just covered with water, over a slow fire for 25-30 minutes. This is called the slow boil method. This method requires more observation and the occasional stir to ensure that the ingredients do not stick to the bottom of the pan.

SPICY BARBECUED MEAT

Originating from the Fujian province in China, barbecued meat or bak kwa is a Hokkien delicacy. My mother-in-law loves bak kwa, so I figured I would make it for her rather than spend hours in a queue to buy it just before Chinese New Year. Mum, this one is for you!

1.5 kg (3.3 lbs) minced lean
    pork
200 g (7 oz) streaky bacon,
    minced

Marinade
2 tablespoons honey
2 tablespoons light soya sauce
2 tablespoons dark caramel soya
    sauce
150 g brown sugar
3 tablespoons Chinese Shaoxing
    rice wine
½ tablespoon salt
1 teaspoon five-spice powder
1½ teaspoon chilli powder or
    2 tablespoons Lingams chilli
    sauce

Mix all the ingredients together well in a bowl and let it sit in the fridge overnight.

Lay the mixture on parchment paper or grease-proof paper and flatten the meat out as thinly as possible. Thereafter, place another sheet on top and use a roller to even out the flattened meat.

There are two methods of drying the meat. One is to dry it in the sun for about 4 hours until the meat can be lifted off the plastic sheet and cut into segments.

The second is to preheat your oven to 180°C (356°F). Put the flattened pork in trays and place it in the oven, with the convection fan switched on, for 10-15 minutes until the meat can be lifted off the trays and cut into segments.

Similarly there are two cooking methods. You can grill the meat over a charcoal fire. Alternatively, put the meat on the top griller of an oven set at 230°C (450°F) and grill each side for 6-7 minutes.

AJ's Notes: I usually get the butcher to grind the bacon with the lean pork. It saves me a lot of time and work. The dark caramel soya sauce gives the barbecued meat its characteristic red.

SEAFOOD

CRAB CURRY

This dish is known as Gulai Ketam in Malay. The term gulai refers to the rich, spicy, savory and succulent gravy in cuisines of Indonesia or Malaysia. A form of curry, it's main ingredient could be meat, fish or crustaceans.

3 swimmer crabs (flower crabs) or Crucifix Crab (*Charybdis Feriatus*), approximately 400 g (14 oz) each
4 tablespoons oil
1 root-end lemongrass (serai), bruised
½ teaspoon palm sugar (gula Melaka)
1 cup coconut cream mixed with ½ cup warm water
½ large white onion, diced
1 slice dried 'tamarind' (assam gelugor, assam keping)
2 turmeric (kunyit) leaves, torn into pieces
Salt to taste

Blended together
½ cup grated coconut,
10 dried chillies, pre-soaked in warm water
10 small shallots
2 root-ends lemongrass (serai)
5 cm (2 in) ginger
3 candlenuts (buah keras)
1 slice dried 'tamarind' (assam gelugor, assam keping)

Heat oil and fry the blended ingredients until fragrant. Add in the bruised lemongrass and palm sugar, and continue frying.

Put in the crabs, coconut milk, onion plus the additional 'tamarind' slice. Allow the crabs to cook, stirring the contents from the bottom up to turn them over until done.

Add the turmeric leaves and salt to taste before serving.

AJ's Note: For how to prepare crabs, see page 13.

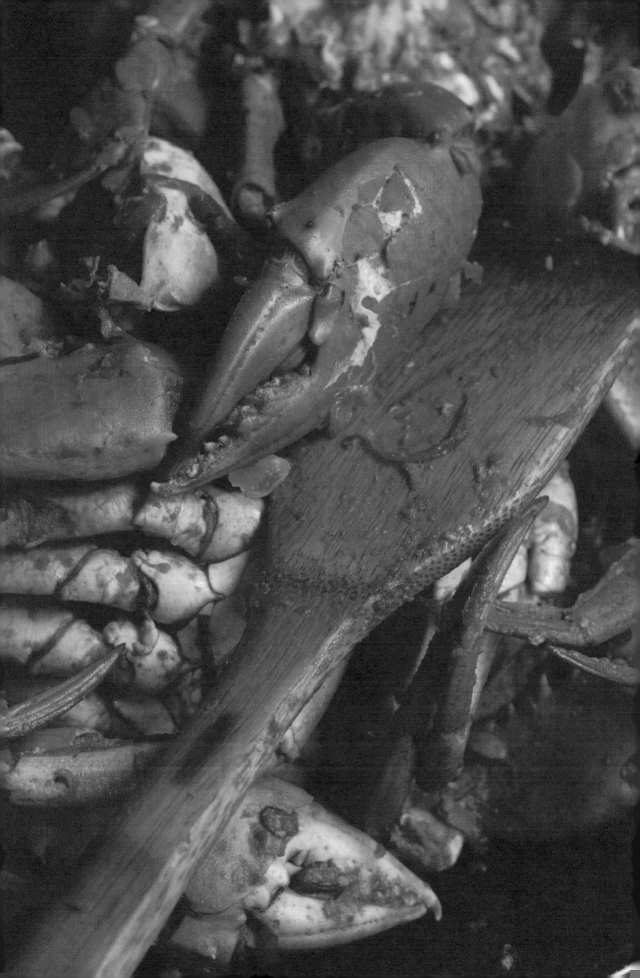

SWEET AND SOUR CRAB WITH CHILLI PADI

Growing up by the sea, this recipe came about when I got home one day with a few rock crabs that I had caught. I looked in the fridge and used the ingredients I found in it.

4 medium rock crabs,
  approximately 800 g (1.7 lbs)
  each
4 tablespoons oil
2 large red onions, chopped
10 cloves garlic, chopped
7.5 cm (3 in) fresh ginger,
  minced
2 tablespoon preserved soya
  beans (taucheo), pounded
15 green bird's eye chillies
  (chilli padi), sliced
10 red bird's eye chillies
  (chilli padi), sliced
Juice from 4 calamansi limes
  (limau kesturi)
2½ teaspoons palm sugar
  (gula Melaka)
1 kaffir lime, grated for rind

Heat oil and brown the onions, garlic and ginger until soft.

Add the preserved soya beans and green and red bird's eye chillies. If the mixture is too thick, add in ½ cup hot water, a little at a time, to obtain a thick gravy-like consistancy. You do not want it watery as the crabs will release water.

Mix well, and add in the calamansi juice and palm sugar. Stir in, taste and adjust for sweet and sourness to your preference. Now put in the crabs, tossing them in the sauce until coated. Cover the pan and turn up heat for 5 minutes.

Remove cover, and toss, bringing the ingredients from the bottom to the top. Reduce the heat and simmer until the shells are bright orange. Garnish with a little grated kaffir lime rind.

AJ's Notes: See page 13 for how to prepare rock crabs.

CHOBADAK

A tea time snack, this sweet potato patty with prawn and coconut filling always hits the spot.

Filling
½ kg (1.1 lbs) prawns, cleaned
   and chopped to a paste
4 tablespoons oil
½ large red onion, chopped
1 red chilli, finely diced
½ cup grated coconut
½ teaspoon salt

Ground together
1 root-end lemongrass (serai)
1 teaspoon fennel powder
5 shallots, finely diced
3 teaspoons chilli paste
1 teaspoon turmeric powder

Dough
½ kg sweet potatoes, boiled,
   skinned and mashed
1 cup of plain flour

Heat oil in a pan and fry ground ingredients until fragrant. Add in prawns, chopped onion and diced chilli. Once the prawns turn orange, add in the coconut and salt. Taste and adjust seasoning to suit yourself. Set aside to cool.

To make the dough, place the mashed sweet potatoes in a mixing bowl and add in the flour while kneading. Make portions the size of a billiard ball, then flatten them in your palms.

Use a spoon and place some pre-cooked filling in the middle of the dough and gently mold the dough into a cutlet/patty.

Heat 2 tablespoons of oil in a pan, and sear each side until brown.

STUFFED SQUID

6 medium-sized squids,

Stuffing
2 tablespoons oil
2 cloves garlic, chopped finely
10 tiger prawns, shelled and chopped finely
6 shitake mushrooms, diced
8 water chestnuts, chopped finely
1 cup cooked rice
2 red chillies, chopped finely
2 stalks spring onions, chopped finely
2 teaspoons soya sauce
1 tablespoon sesame oil
¼ teaspoon pepper

Sauce
4 tablespoons hoisin sauce
1 tablespoon chilli sauce
1 tablespoon sweet dark soya sauce
4 bird's eye chilli (chilli padi)
½ cup hot water

To prepare the stuffing, heat oil and fry the garlic until it is light brown, then add in the chopped prawns. After 2-3 minutes, add in the diced mushrooms and simmer another 2-3 minutes before turning off the heat. Now combine with the remaining stuffing ingredients nicely. Set aside to cool.

Spoon the mixture into the individual squids, leaving about 2½ cm (1 in) of space at the opening. Push the ends of the longer tentacles into the opening, then replace the head of the squid. Using two toothpicks, seal the opening with an X, basically piercing the skin, through the head and out the other side of the neck. Repeat for remaning squids and stuffing.

Prepare the sauce by combining the ingredients.

Heat 2 tablespoons of oil in a non-stick pan that has a lid. Place the squids, three at a time, into the pan and fry. Cover the pan to prevent getting splattered by hot oil as you fry.

Once cooked, slice the squid into 1½ cm (½ in) rings. Pour the sauce over and serve.

AJ's Notes: To prepare the squid, remove the membrane and head from the body Discard the eyes and beak from the head. Keep the head for cooking. When using dried shitake mushrooms, soak them in hot water before dicing.

DRY, SPICY FRIED CRABS

3 swimmer crabs (flower crabs)
   or Crucifix Crab (*Charybdis*
   Feriatus), approximately 400 g
   (14 oz) each
2 heaped tablespoons clarified
   butter (ghee)
1 chicken stock cube
Juice from 1 calamansi lime
   (limau kesturi)
2 cups thin coconut milk
½ teaspoon salt
½ teaspoon brown sugar
½ cup thick coconut milk
2 sprigs coriander leaves,
   chopped

Roasted together and ground
2 teaspoon cumin seeds
   (jintan putih)
2 tablespoons black peppercorns
5 cm (2 in) cinnamon stick
4 cloves
1 teaspoon fennel seeds
   (jintan manis)
1½ star anise
2 tablespoons grated coconut
3 tablespoons poppy seeds
   (kas-kas)

Spices
15 green chillies, sliced
20 spring onions, sliced
4 cloves garlic
2 cm (¾ in) turmeric, diced
2 sprigs curry leaves

Combine the ground ingredients with the spices. Heat the ghee and fry the spice mixture until fragrant. Stir well, then add the chicken stock cube, lime juice, thin coconut milk and bring to a boil.

Add the crabs, salt, sugar and mix well. Reduce the heat to medium low and cover pan cooking until crabs are done, about 15 minutes.

Remove cover, now slowly add in the thick coconut milk, stir and switch off the heat as soon as the mixture starts to boil. Garnish with the coriander leaves.

AJ's Note: See page 13 for the method of preparing and cleaning crabs.

THAI-STYLE FRIED CRABS

3 swimmer crabs (flower crabs)
  or Crucifix Crab (*Charybdis
  Feriatus*), approximately 400 g
  (14 oz) each
2 eggs
1½ tablespoons Thai chilli paste
  (Nam Prik Pao)
1 cup coconut milk
3 tablespoons oil
1½ cm (1 in) galangal
  (lengkuas), minced
5 cm (2 in) fresh ginger, minced
1 clove garlic, chopped
2 cups chicken stock
3 tablespoons fish sauce
2 teaspoon palm sugar
  (gula Melaka)
2 teaspoons curry powder
2 stalks spring onions, diced
2 red chillies, halved lengthwise
  and deseeded
2 sprigs coriander leaves,
  chopped coarsely
1 small red onion, wedged
½ teaspoon grated kaffir lime
  rind

Beat the eggs with the chilli paste and coconut milk until smooth. Leave aside.

Heat the oil in a frying pan, lower heat and fry the galangal and garlic until light brown. Add in the crabs followed by stock, fish sauce, palm sugar and curry powder. Bring to the boil.

When the sauce is reduced to half, add in the spring onions, red chillies and coriander leaves and red onion wedges. Stir well.

When the crabs are orange, add in the beaten egg mixture. Mix and simmer for 2 minutes, then remove immediately from heat. Continue to stir and mix in the grated kaffir lime rind.

AJ's Note: See page 13 for the method of preparing and cleaning crabs.

SQUID, FISH AND PRAWNS WITH BASIL (RIGHT)

100 g (3.5 oz) squid, cut into
   thick rings
200 g (7 oz) garoupa or snapper
   fillets, cut into bite-sized pieces
10 large prawns, shelled
2 fresh red chillies, diced
3 coriander roots, chopped
3 tablespoons oil
2 tablespoons oyster sauce
2 tablespoons fish sauce
1 red pepper, sliced lengthwise
6 bird's eye chilli (chilli padi),
   chopped
6 sprigs spring onions, white
   ends only, chopped
1 teaspoon palm sugar
   (gula Melaka)
½ cup basil leaves, shredded

Grind or pound the red chillies and coriander root into a paste.

Heat the oil, add the paste, and cook until fragrant. Now, put in the seafood and stir-fry until tender, then in sequence stir in the sauces, pepper, bird's eye chilli, spring onions, palm sugar and basil leaves.

Cook for another 5 minutes and serve.

AJ's Notes: Squid and prawns provide a unique flavour to this dish. You could replace the fish with crab meat and add scallops.

WHITEBAIT CURRY

1 cup dried whitebait (ikan bilis)
4 tomatoes, skinned and
   chopped
2 potatoes, skinned and cubed
1 stalk curry leaves
½ cup thick coconut milk
1 cup of hot water
Juice from 6 calamansi limes
   (limau kesturi)
Salt and sugar to taste
Oil for frying

Ground together
8 shallots or 1 large red onion
2 cloves garlic
2½ cm (1 in) ginger
4 candlenuts (buah keras)
5 fresh red chillies
2 bird's eye chillies (chilli padi)
1 teaspoon turmeric powder

Heat up 4 tablespoons oil, and when hot, lightly fry the whitebait for about 2 minutes till they are slightly crispy. Set aside.

In the same oil, fry the ground ingredients until aromatic, then drop in the chopped tomatoes.

Once the tomatoes have broken down, add in the potatoes, curry leaves, coconut milk and water. Allow to simmer for 6 minutes until the potatoes are almost done.

Now, add in the whitebait then stir gently while adding in the calamansi juice. Finally, season with sugar and salt to taste.

DAD'S BAKED STINGRAY (LEFT)

My dad's creation, this recipe has been a family favourite for as long as I can remember. The first secret is in the way the fish is marinated, and the second is in the magical sambal pencuri sauce (see below) which this dish must be served with. You will embark on a journey of flavours when you taste this dish. Pencuri *means 'thief' in Malay. The legend goes that a pregnant woman kept sneaking into her mother's kitchen to taste this sambal, upon which the mother yelled: "Si-apa curi sambal?" (Who is stealing the sambal?), and so the name evolved.*

4 medium-sized slices stingray
3 calamansi limes (limau kesturi)
¼ teaspoon salt
1 teaspoon turmeric powder
½ teaspoon chilli powder
8 turmeric leaves

Squeeze the lime juice over the fish, then season with salt. Set aside. Pour the lime juice from the fish into a bowl, and add the turmeric and chilli powder to form a paste. Massage it on the stingray slices and marinate for 2 hours.

Heat the turmeric leaves over the stove to soften, and use 2 pieces to wrap each slice of fish, sealing ends with toothpicks.

Bake in a moderate oven of 150 °C (302°F) for about 25 minutes or until a skewer goes into the fish easily.

AJ's Note: It is from here that I learnt to use lime on fish to remove odor and traces of blood from the gills.

SAMBAL PENCURI

2 golf-ball-sized tamarind paste
   (assam jawa) mixed in 2 cups
   hot water
15 shallots, thinly sliced
1 torch ginger bud (bunga
   kantan), chopped finely
1 tablespoon shrimp paste
   (belacan), toasted till fragrant
Juice from 8 calamansi limes
   (limau kesturi)
2 tablespoons sugar
½ teaspoon salt to taste
10 bird's eye chilli (chilli padi),
   sliced thinly
3 red chillies, deseeded and
   diced

Sieve the thick tamarind liquid into a mixing bowl. Mix in all the remaining ingredients and stir. Serve with the baked stingray.

FISH MOOLIE

I always think of my mum when I make this gem of a dish from the shores of Kerala as it is one of her favourite dishes. Fishing is a favourite pastime of mine, and this is one dish that is perfect with line-caught fish.

1 fish, approximately 900 g
   (2 lbs), garoupa (kerapu),
   snapper (jenahak), tiger-
   toothed croaker (tengkerong),
   or parrot fish (bayan)
2 tablespoons water
1½ teaspoons turmeric powder
½ teaspoon salt
¼ teaspoon pepper
4 tablespoons oil
6 shallots, sliced
4 slices young ginger, shredded
1 cup thin coconut milk
1 cup thick coconut milk
2 tablespoons white vinegar
4 camias (*Averrhoa Bilimbi*,
   belimbing asam), halved
   lengthwise
2 kaffir lime leaves
¼ teaspoon mustard seeds
¼ teaspoon black pepper

Pounded together
1 root-end lemongrass (serai)
2½ cm (1 in) fresh turmeric or
   1½ teaspoons turmeric powder
4 candlenuts (buah keras)
2 green chillies
4 bird's eye chilli (chilli padi)

Garnish
Fried onions
2½ cm (1 inch) young ginger,
   shredded
1 clove garlic, shredded
Green chillies, deseeded and
   shredded

Mix the water, turmeric powder, salt, and pepper and massage on and inside the fish (belly and gill area as well) and fry in oil till golden. Remove the fish and set aside.

Heat the same oil again and fry the sliced shallots and ginger until soft but not brown. Add in the pounded ingredients and fry until golden. Now add in the thin coconut milk, keeping the heat low.

Once simmering, add the thick coconut milk and give it a few stirs before adding the vinegar, belimbing, kaffir lime leaves, mustard seeds and black pepper. The gravy should be not too thick but creamy in texture. Slide in the fried fish. Simmer for 5 minutes, garnish, and serve.

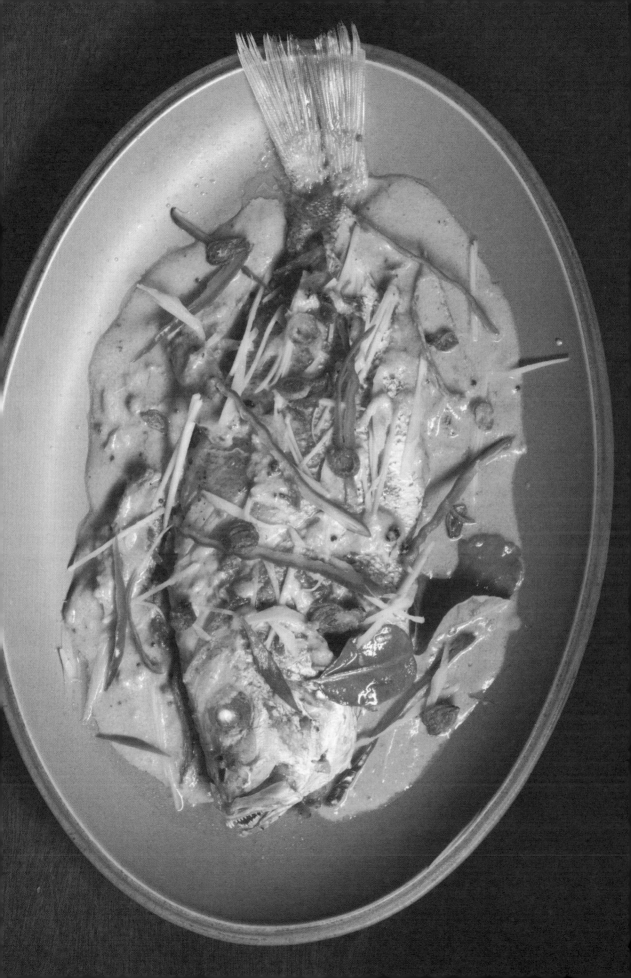

POOR MAN'S PRAWNS

I must have been about 19-20 years old. I had gone fishing with a few friends at an old kelong off the Johor Straits and befriended a prawn fisherman. At the time, bartering was common and coming from a humble background, I did not have much money. So, I traded a couple of my fish (I think they were Grunters, gerut-gerut) for a small bag of prawns. When I got home later, I rummaged through the fridge for ingredients and created this dish.

Most of the time when I cook, I find simplicity in the ingredients often bring out the rarest gems. Like friendship, you can never know when you will meet the rarest of true friends. I cooked this dish for one such rare gem on her birthday. Thank you Anita for your friendship, and God bless you always.

½ kg (1.1 lbs) prawns
2 tablespoons oil
½ teaspoon pepper
10 Thai basil leaves, chopped
4 tablespoons oil
3 teaspoons brown sugar
10 basil leaves
4 bird's eye chillies (chilli padi), sliced

Blended together
5 red chillies
2½ cm (1 in) ginger
2 cloves garlic
10 Thai basil leaves
3 teaspoons preseved soya beans (taucheong)
2 bird's eye chillies (chilli padi)

Remove sacs from the prawn heads and veins on the backs, leaving shells on. (See page 12 for detailed method of cleaning prawns.)

Place the prawns in a mixing bowl and add in the oil, pepper and chopped basil leaves. Allow to marinade for 1–2 hours in the fridge.

Heat the oil in a pan and fry the blended ingredients until aromatic. Stir the brown sugar into the gravy, adding ½ cup of water a little at a time if the ingredients are too dry. Now put in the prawns and stir to ensure they are evenly coated.

Cover and cook for about 6 minutes until the prawns are bright orange. Turn off the heat, include the basil leaves and mix nicely. Finally, toss in the sliced bird's eye chillies, and the dish is ready to be served.

MY BAKED STINGRAY

This is my variation of Dad's Baked Stingray preparation. The Sambal Pencuri from the original recipe is now Sambal I-Curi. Curi in Malay means steal.

4 medium-sized slices stingray
3 calamansi limes (limau kesturi)
¼ teaspoon salt
1 teaspoon turmeric powder
1½ teaspoon Thai chilli paste
    (Nam Prik Pao)
8 turmeric leaves

Squeeze lime juice over the fish, then season with salt. Set aside. In a bowl, mix the turmeric and Thai chilli paste. Massage it into the stingray slices and marinate for 2 hours.

Heat the turmeric leaves over the stove fire to soften them, and wrap each slice of fish with two leaves, sealing both ends with toothpicks.

Bake the packets of fish in a moderate oven of 150 °C (302°F) for about 25 minutes or until a skewer goes into the fish easily.

SAMBAL I-CURI

2 golf-ball-sized tamarind paste
    (assam jawa) mixed in 2 cups
    hot water
15 shallots, thinly sliced
1 torch ginger bud (bunga
    kantan), chopped finely
Grated rind from 1 kaffir lime
2 kaffir lime leaves, middle rib
    removed, finely diced
1 tablespoon shrimp paste
    (belacan), toasted till fragrant
Juice from 8 calamansi limes
    (limau kesturi)
Rind from 2 calamansi limes,
    diced
2 tablespoons palm sugar
    (gula Melaka)
1 teaspoon black vinegar
10 red bird's eye chilli
    (chilli padi), sliced thinly
5 green bird's eye chilli (chilli
    padi), sliced thinly
1 tablespoon fried shallots

Pour the thick tamarind liquid through a sieve into a mixing bowl. Mix in all the remaining ingredients and stir. Serve with the baked stingray.

AJ's Notes: It is always a matter of time before any recipe evolves, and I know a time will come when my son, Brad, tastes my Sambal I-Curi and makes his own Sambal Di-curi (stolen).

FISH HEAD ASSAM PEDAS

1 garoupa or snapper head,
  approximately 1 kg (2.2 lbs),
  cut into 8 pieces
2 tablespoons turmeric powder
1½ teaspoons salt
1 teaspoon pepper
8 ladies fingers (okra), halved
2 brinjals, quartered
Oil for deep frying
1 rounded tablespoon tamarind,
  mixed with 1 cup water
2 torch ginger buds (bunga
  kantan), one halved and one
  chopped finely
12 sprigs Vietnamese coriander
  (laksa leaves, daun kesum)
2 tomatoes, quartered
1 large red onion, quartered
2 green chillies, cut lengthwise
2 slices dried 'tamarind' (asam
  gelugor, assam keping)
3 teaspoons sugar
Salt to taste

Ground together
20 dried chillies, pre-soaked in
  hot water
2 fresh red chillies
2 large red onions
6 candlenuts (buah keras)
2½ cm (1 in) turmeric or
  1 teaspoon turmeric powder
4 cloves garlic
2 root-ends of lemongrass (serai)

Garnish
Mint leaves
Coriander leaves
Sliced onions

Season the fish head with the turmeric powder, salt, and pepper and deep fry in a wok till golden. This is essential as the frying will seal the fish and will ensure that the fish head does not break up. Remove the fish head and set aside.

Now fry the ladies fingers and the brinjals. Once cooked, remove and place with the fish head.

Remove all but 10 tablespoons of oil in the pan. In this oil, fry the ground ingredients until oil rises to the top. Add in tamarind liquid plus another 1½ cups water. Bring to the boil. Now add the torch ginger, chopped up pieces as well as the halves, and Vietnamese coriander leaves. Boil.

Once the gravy is bubbling, put in the fried fish head, tomatoes, onion and green chillies, 'tamarind' slices and sugar. Check and adjust for salt, then return the ladies fingers and brinjals to the pan. Garnish and serve.

BLACK PEPPER CRABS

3 rock crabs, approximately
  800 g (1.8 lbs) each
¼ cup of Chinese rice wine
  (Shaoxing rice wine)
180 g (6 oz) butter
3 cloves garlic, chopped
3 cm (1½ in) ginger, chopped
2 teaspoons dried prawns,
  roasted and chopped finely
6 shallots, diced
2 sprigs curry leaves
1 tablespoon chillie paste
3 tablespoons freshly ground
  black peppercorns
1 teaspoon light soya sauce
1 tablespoon oyster sauce
1 tablespoon red date dark sauce
½ cup dark soya sauce
1½ teaspoons brown sugar
½ cup chicken stock

Garnish
1 sprig spring onions, chopped
A few coriander leaves, plucked

Heat a dry wok with the Chinese rice wine. Once sizzling, turn up the heat and pour in the crabs. Toss the crabs and sear them until the wine vaporises. Take out the crabs and set aside. The crabs should be semi-cooked.

In the same wok, melt the butter over low heat. Once melted, add in the garlic, ginger and dried prawns and cook till brown. Now add in the shallots, curry leaves, chilli paste, black pepper, light soya, oyster, red date sauce, dark soya sauce and brown sugar. Once you have a thick consistency, add in the chicken stock and bring to a boil.

Put the crabs back into the pan. Simmer on high, turning the crabs for 8-10 minutes until they are coated and cooked.

AJ's Notes: See page 13 for the preparation of rock crabs. This recipe can also be used for king prawns cooked with shells on, green mussels, lobsters or squids.

Red Date Thick Soya Sauce (Toong Foong Sauce Factory - Longevity god brand) is available at most supermarkets in Southeast Asia.

PANDAN FISH (RIGHT)

440 g (1 lb) fish fillet, cut into
   16 cubes
8 fresh shitake mushrooms,
   halved
16 pandanus (pandan) leaves

Mixed together
½ cup chicken stock
¼ cup coconut milk
2 teaspoons cornflour
2 sprigs coriander leaves, finely
   diced
2 teaspoons fish sauce
1 large red onion, finely diced
1 tablespoon curry powder
1 tablespoon sesame oil
¼ teaspoon turmeric powder
¼ teaspoon palm sugar
   (gula Melaka)
¼ teaspoon black peppercorns,
   crushed

Combine all the ingredients for the mixture in a bowl, stir in and mix well. Now add in the fish and the shitake mushrooms, ensuring all are coated well. Set aside and allow to marinate for about an hour.

To prepare the fish packets, lay a pandan leaf with one end towards you. Place a cube of fish at one end of the leaf and a piece of shitake on the fish. Roll the leaf up to enclose the fish. You will basically have a cylindrical shape. Pierce bamboo toothpicks at both ends to seal the packet. Repeat for remaining fish and leaves.

Pre-heat a pan or wok with ½ cup of oil. When hot, fry the packets till the fish is cooked.

AJ's Notes: If the pandanus leaves are large, use eight and cut each into two. My favourite dipping sauce for this dish is Sambal Kicap Manis (see below). It takes only 5 minutes to prepare.

SAMBAL KICAP MANIS

1 cup sweet soy sauce,
   ABC Kicap Manis preferred
Juice from 8 calamansi limes
   (limau kesturi)
Rind from 2 calamansi limes,
   diced
1 tablespoons palm sugar
½ teaspoon salt
10 bird's eye chilli (chilli padi),
   sliced thinly
1 clove garlic, diced
5 shallots, diced

Mix all the ingredients and the sauce is ready.

THREE SEASONINGS FOR ALMOND FISH

These recipes are for searing, griddle, oven or open grill style of cooking. They can be prepared with fish slices, steaks or fillets from cod, salmon, mackerel (tenggiri), snapper, tuna (tongkol), bonito or wahoo.

4 slices of fish of your choice
Flour for coating fish
2 egg whites
Chopped almonds for coating
1 lemon, for juice

Asian seasoning
1 tablespoon ginger juice
1 teaspoon garlic juice obtained
   by blending fresh garlic
1¼ tablespoons light soya sauce
1 tablespoon sesame oil
1 teaspoon pepper

Mediterranean seasoning
1 tablespoon butter
2 garlic cloves, ground
2 teaspoons paprika
1 teaspoon ground black pepper

Italian seasoning
2 garlic cloves, ground
1 tablespoon butter
1 tablespoon Italian spice herb
   mix (basil, marjoram, oregano,
   rosemary, thyme) or fresh
   basil, cilantro (coriander),
   rosemary and a little sage
   chopped up together

Use one of the three seasoning ingredients to marinate the fish for 10 minutes.

Dip the fish in flour, then the beaten egg white and almond mixture. Shallow fry or grill or sear until golden. Squeeze some lemon juice over fried fish before serving.

THAI PRAWN HORS D'OEUVRES

½ kg (1.1 lbs) prawns, shelled
1 bunch of betel leaves (daun
  kadok) or butter lettuce leaves

Filling
1½ cups grated coconut, roasted
  until light brown
12 shallots, diced and fried till
  golden
Pulp of 6 large limes, diced
7½ cm (3 in) ginger, diced
3 tablespoons dried shrimps,
  toasted then chopped
6 bird's eye chillies (chilli padi),
  chopped
3 tablespoons unsalted roasted
  peanuts or almonds, chopped

Sauce
2½ cm (1 in) galangal (lengkuas)
170 g (6 oz) palm sugar
  (gula Melaka)
2½ tablespoons fish sauce
2½ cups water

Blanch the prawns in hot water for 2 minutes. Drain and set the prawns aside.

Boil the sauce ingredients together and simmer until reduced to about 1½ cups. Allow to cool.

Mix the chopped ingredients and nuts to make the filling.

Put a leaf in your palm. Place a blanched prawn in the centre and top with a tablespoon of the filling with some of the sauce. Roll up and eat.

STEAMED FISH TEOCHEOW STYLE

The Teochew or Chaozhou Chinese people come from the Chaoshan region of eastern Guang-dong which borders the South China Sea. Therefore, they love eating fresh fish – especially pomfret – and are particular about how it is prepared. In Southeast Asia, we have a wide choice of other fish suitable for steaming, including threadfin (senangin), stingray (pari), garoupa (ker-apu), spotted snapper (jenahak) and parrot fish (bayan).

1 sea bass (siakap), approximately 700 g (1.5 lbs)
1 calamansi lime
1½ teaspoons sugar
1 cup clear chicken stock or 1 chicken cube dissolved in 1 cup water
2 teaspoons sesame oil
1 sprig coriander leaves, chopped.

Seasoning
2 leaves salted vegetable (kiam chye), soaked in water and sliced thinly
2 root-ends lemongrass (serai), bruised
4 kaffir lime leaves (daun limau perut)
4 preserved garlic bulbs, halved
8 bird's eye chillies (chillie padi), halved lengthwise
4 preserved sour plum, smashed lightly

Gut and clean the fish, (or have your fishmonger do it). Pat the fish dry with a kitchen towel. Make two diagonal slits on both sides of the fish and season with salt and pepper.

Now, turn the fish belly up over the sink and squeeze in the juice of the calamansi lime and rub in the juices starting from the gills, down the spine into the belly. This makes a very big difference in steamed fish.

Place the prepared fish in a steaming dish. Arrange the seasoning ingredients on top and around the fish. Mix the sugar with the stock and pour over the fish. Now drizzle the sesame oil over. Steam until done, about 10-12 minutes. Taste for seasoning and adjust if necessary. Garnish.

AJ's Note: See page 13 for the timing of steaming fish.

STINGRAY ASSAM PEDAS

2 pieces of stingray, approx 1 kg
(2.2 lbs), cut into 4 inch
(10 cm) wedges
2 tablespoons turmeric powder
1½ teaspoons salt
1 teaspoon pepper
6 tablespoons oil
1 tin pineapple rings (approximately 10 rings), use 8, keep
2 for blending (see below)
1 golf-ball-sized tamarind,
mixed in 1 cup water
2 torch ginger buds (bunga
kantan), one halved and one
chopped finely
2 tomatoes, quartered
12 sprigs Vietnamese coriander
(laksa leaves, daun kesum),
leaves only
3 teaspoons palm sugar
(gula Melaka)
Salt to taste

Blended together
20 dried chillies, pre-soaked in
hot water
2 fresh red chillies
2 fresh green chillies
15 shallots
6 candlenuts (buah keras)
2½ cm (1 in) fresh turmeric
4 cloves garlic
2 root ends lemongrass (serai)
2 pineapple rings
2 slices dried 'tamarind' (asam
gelugor, assam keping)
15 leaves Vietnamese coriander
(laksa leaves, daun kesum)

Garnish
Mint leaves
Fried sliced onions

Season the stingray with the turmeric powder, salt, and pepper.

Pre-heat a pan with oil and, when hot, lightly fry the stingray until golden. This is essential as the frying will seal the fish and ensure that the meat does not break up. Remove the fish and set aside.

In the same oil, fry 8 pineapple rings. Once cooked, remove and place with the fish pieces.

In the remaining oil, fry the blended ingredients until oil rises. Add in tamarind liquid plus another 1½ cups of water. Bring to the boil. Now add the torch ginger, tomatoes and Vietnamese coriander leaves and simmer to a boil.

Once the gravy is bubbling, put in the fried fish pieces, pineapple and palm sugar. Check and adjust for salt. Garnish and serve.

RAJOO'S CRAB CURRY

I named this dish after my godson, Andre, who told me this little Malaysian joke. Andre: "Godpa, how do you spell 'Raju'? Me: R.A.J.U. Andre: "No Godpa, its Rrrrrrr Yaaaaaa Jaaaaaaa Woo Woo." This one is for you, Andre. You're the best godson ever!

3 swimmer crabs (flower crabs) or Crucifix Crab (*Charybdis Feriatus*), approximately 400 g (14 oz) each
4 tablespoons oil
1 teaspoon Indian five-spice mix (panch poran)
4 tablespoons fish curry powder
2 tablespoons chilli paste
1 heaped tablespoon tamarind (assam), mixed in ½ cup water
7½ cm (3 in) ginger, sliced thickly and bruised
Juice from 5 calamansi limes (limau kesturi)
½ teaspoon brown sugar
¼ teaspoon salt
¼ teaspoon pepper
1 cup drumstick leaves for thickening the curry
2 teaspoon cumin seeds (jintan putih), dry fried and pounded

Blended together
2 large red onions
5 cloves garlic
2 stalks curry leaves, leaves only
6 red chillies

Heat oil and fry the 5-spice mix until aromatic. Add the blended ingredients and fry until the oil rises. Put in the fish curry powder and chilli paste and mix well.

Add the crabs, mix nicely to coat with the mixture then add in 1½ cups of hot water. Include the tamarind liquid and the sliced, bruised ginger.

When the crabs are cooked, add in the lime juice, sugar, salt and pepper. Now put in the drumstick leaves, mixing nicely. The leaves will make the gravy cling to the crabs. Switch off the heat and sprinkle the dry fried pounded cumin powder over crabs.

AJ's Notes: Panch poran is a simple mixture of spices that you can prepare and keep in a small jar ready for use. The spices are not powdered but whole. They are: 1 tablespoon each of mustard seeds, fenugreek, cumin seeds, fennel seeds and white dhall. Some variations use onion seeds (kalonji) in place of white dhall.

CURRY LADA

A wide range of fish can be used for this curry: Threadfin (senangin), mackerel (tenggiri), stingray (pari), tuna (tongkol), garoupa (kerapu), spotted snapper (jenahak) and sea bass (siakap).

1 kg (2.2 lbs) fish, cut into serving pieces
1 round purple brinjal, quartered and/or 6 ladies fingers (okra), halved
1 golf-ball-sized tamarind paste mixed in 1 cup water
Palm sugar (gula Melaka) to taste
Salt to taste

Ground together
1½ tablespoons white peppercorns
1½ tablespoons cumin (jintan putih)
1½ tablespoons chilli paste
1 tablespoon turmeric powder
10 shallots or 2 large red onions
4 cloves garlic
1¼ cm (½ in) shrimp paste (belacan), cut widthwise from a 10 x 5 x 5 cm (5 x 2 x 2 in) block, toasted

Heat up 4 tablespoons oil and lightly fry the brinjal and/or the ladies fingers. Set aside.

In the same oil, fry the ground ingredients until fragrant and the oil rises. Then add in the tamarind liquid, slowly stirring and bring to a boil. Taste and adjust to your preference of sourness and pepperiness by adding more tamarind liquid and pepper. Put in sugar and salt to taste

Include the fish, brinjal and/or ladies fingers, cover lid and cook until done. The cooking time is 10-12 minutes; turn the fish over at the 6 minute mark.

STUFFED FRIED FISH

6 scomber (kembung) or
   torpedo scad (cencaru)
8 calamansi limes (limau kesturi)
½ teaspoon palm sugar
   (gula Melaka)
1 tablespoon turmeric powder
½ teaspoon salt
½ teaspoon pepper

Pounded together
5 fresh chillies
3 bird's eye chillies (chilli padi)
8 shallots
2½ cm (1 in) shrimp paste
   (belacan), cut widthwise from
   a 10 x 5 x 5 cm (5 x 2 x 2 in)
   block
1½ tablespoons dried prawns,
   soaked in warm water
4 candlenuts (buah keras)
½ teaspoon salt
½ teaspoon pepper

Remove the gills, and gut the fish (or have your fishmonger do it). Pat the fish dry with a kitchen towel. Turn the fish belly up and squeeze the juice of the 4 calamansi limes on the fish and rub in the juices starting from the gills, down the spine and into the belly. Use the tumeric powder, salt and pepper to coat the fish. Set aside.

Fry the pounded ingredients and add the palm sugar to the mixture. Dish out this spice mix to cool. When the spice mixture is cool, use it to fill the fish head and belly, reserving the extra filling.

Shallow fry the fish until crispy. Remove the fish and place on a serving dish, leaving on low heat on to keep the oil hot. Put the left-over filling on the fish, squeeze lime juice from the remaining 4 limes over, and spoon some of the hot oil on the fish.

AJ's Notes: Here is a variation of the pounded ingredients for stuffing:

6 fresh chillies,
3 bird's eye chillies (chilli padi)
8 shallots
1½ tablespoons dried prawns, toasted
½ cup grated coconut
½ torch ginger bud (bunga kantan), chopped
1 root-end lemongrass (serai), chopped
½ teaspoon salt
½ teaspoon pepper

THAI GREEN CURRY CRABS

4 swimmer crabs (flower crabs)
   or Crucifix Crab (*Charybdis
   Feriatus*), approximately 400 g
   (14 oz) each or 4 medium
   rock crabs, approximately 800
   g (1.7 lbs) each
½ cup thick coconut cream
1 teaspoon palm sugar
   (gula Melaka)
3 tablespoons fish sauce
2 tablespoons calamansi juice
4 tablespoons oil
2 kaffir lime leaves (daun limau
   perut)
½ cup chicken stock
12 Thai sweet basil leaves
5 green bird's eye chilli
   (chilli padi), optional

Green Curry Paste: blended together
1 root-end lemongrass (serai)
10 green chillies
6 shallots
5 cloves garlic
7.5 cm (3 in) galangal (lengkuas)
½ cup chopped coriander leaves
   and stems
½ cup Thai sweet basil leaves
2 kaffir lime leaves (daun limau
   perut)
½ teaspoon ground cumin,
   roasted
½ teaspoon ground white pepper
½ teaspoon ground coriander,
   roasted
1 teaspoon shrimp paste
   (belacan), roasted
1 teaspoon palm sugar
   (gula Melaka)
1 teaspoon sea salt

Add the green curry paste into a mixing bowl. Add in your crabs, coconut cream, palm sugar, fish sauce and calamansi juice. Mix well and leave to marinade in fridge.

When ready to cook, pre-heat 4 tablespoons of oil in a wok or large frying pan. Add in the crabs and kaffir lime leaves, tossing them in the sauce until coated.

Include the chicken stock, toss and cover the pan. Turn up heat for 5 minutes.

Remove cover, and toss again, bringing the ingredients from the bottom to the top. Reduce the heat and simmer until the shells are bright orange.

Switch off the heat and add in Thai sweet basil leaves and the bird's eye chilli if using. Give it a quick stir and serve.

FISH BAKED WITH PINEAPPLE SLICES

My Mum knows that this recipe completes me in so many ways.

1 red snapper (merah),
   approximately 1.3 kg (2.8 lbs)
1 large can pineapple rings,
   approximately 10 rings
½ cup coconut cream diluted
   with ½ cup water

Ground together
12 dried chillies, soaked in water
3 fresh red chillies
4 bird's eye chillies (chilli padi)
2 large red onions
1 root-end lemongrass (serai)
3 cloves garlic
1½ teaspoon dried prawns,
   toasted
1¼ cm (½ in) shrimp paste
   (belacan), cut widthwise from
   a 10 x 5 x 5 cm (5 x 2 x 2 in)
   block, toasted
4 candlenuts (buah keras)
5 cm (2 in) young ginger
2 pineapple rings, from tin
½ cup pineapple juice from the can
3 petals torch ginger bud (bunga
   kantan)

Garnish
1 petal torch ginger bud (bunga
   kantan), finely diced

Gut and clean the fish, then make one or two slashes on either side of fish.

Place the fish into oven-proof dish and arrange pineapple rings over the fish. Reserve the pineapple juice.

Fry the ground ingredients until fragrant and oil rises. Add the remaining juice from the tinned pineapple and the coconut milk. Mix well. Taste for seasoning – the gravy must be slightly sweet and not watery.

Pour the gravy over the fish and bake in a moderate oven (175°C, 350°F) for about 45 minutes or until done. Indications include the browning of the pineapple, the eyes of the fish turning white and the skewer test where a skewer can easily slide through the fish to the bone.

AJ's Notes: The gravy can be made a day ahead and poured onto fish before baking.

This can be prepared with snapper (pink, striped, spotted or red), garoupa (kerapu), triple tail (pecah periuk), sea bass (siakap) and many other variaties of scaled fish.

STUFFED SHAD

Toli Shad (Sarawak terubok) is highly prized in Southeast Asia for its meat and eggs. Sadly, due to this demand, overfishing has depleted the stock alarmingly, so enjoy this dish once in a long while as a treat.

1 Toli Shad, approximately
   1.3 kg (2.80 lbs)
2 calamansi limes (limau kesturi)
1 tablespoon turmeric powder
6 tablespoons light soya sauce
Oil for deep frying
2½ tablespoons vinegar
1 teaspoon palm sugar
   (gula Melaka)

Pounded together
4 red chillies
8 shallots
4 candlenuts (buah keras)
2½ cm (1 in) shrimp paste
   (belacan), cut widthwise from
   a 10 x 5 x 5 cm (5 x 2 x 2 in)
   block
1½ tablespoons dried prawns,
   soaked in warm water
½ teaspoon salt
½ teaspoon sugar
½ teaspoon white pepper
10 young betel leaves (daun
   kadok), sliced thinly

Remove the gills, and gut the fish by making a small incision to remove the innards (or have your fishmonger do it). Do NOT remove the scales. Pat the fish dry with a kitchen towel. Turn the fish belly up and squeeze the juice of the calamansi lime, rubbing in the juice starting from the gills, down the spine and into the belly.

Holding the head down on the table, pull the tail towards you to dislodge the bones. You will hear a cracking sound as the bones dislodge. You are probably wondering why on earth this is done. Trust me. This makes a very big difference when eating the fish.

Stuff the fish with the pounded ingredients, then rub the fish all over with turmeric powder. Deep fry the fish on low heat, about 8 minutes per side. The scales should be crispy. Remove the fish to a serving plate and drain the oil.

Heat 3 tablespoons of fresh oil in the pan and pour in the light soya sauce, vinegar and 1 tablespoon of palm sugar. Spoon the sauce over the fish and serve immediately.

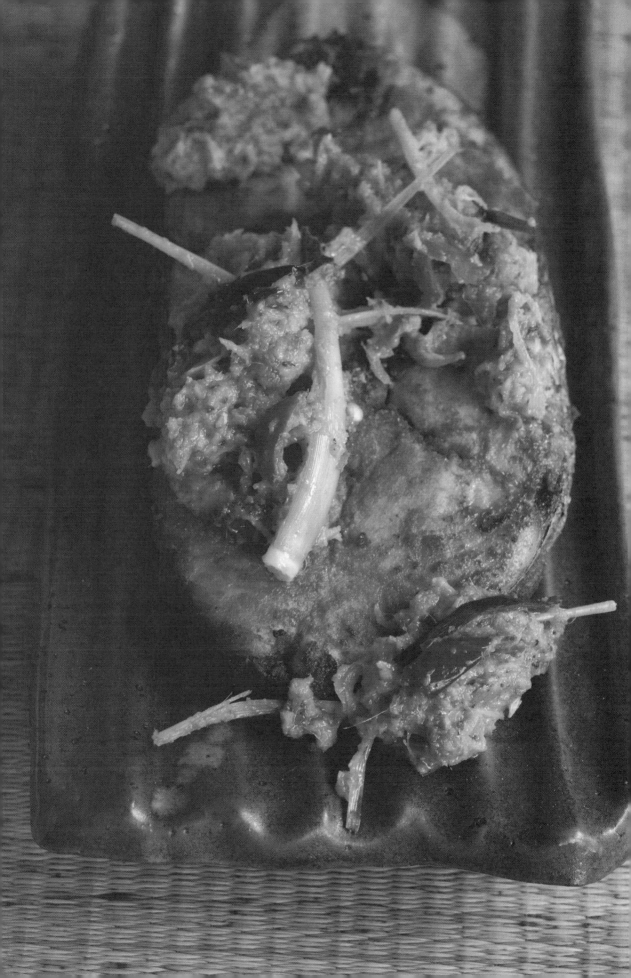

MACKEREL RENDANG

1 kg (2.2 lbs) mackerel slices
4 calamansi limes (limau kesturi)
½ teaspoon salt
½ teaspoon pepper
1 tablespoon turmeric powder
Oil for deep frying
¾ cup coconut milk
½ cup water
3 slices dried 'tamarind' (assam
   gelugor, assam keping)
1 root-end lemongrass (serai)
2 turmeric leaves, shredded
2 tablespoons fried ground
   coconut (kerisik)
Coriander leaves

Ground together
10 bird's eye chillies (chilli padi)
2 large red onions
4 cloves garlic
2 slices ginger
2 slices galangal (lengkuas)
2 tablespoons palm sugar
   (gula Melaka)
1 root-end lemongrass (serai)
½ teaspoon salt

Clean the fish and squeeze the juice of the calamansi lime, rubbing in the juice starting from the gills, down the spine and into the belly. Lay out the fish on a flat surface and season lightly with salt, pepper, calamansi and turmeric powder. Heat the oil and deep fry the fish until just golden and slightly crispy. Move the fish to a serving plate.

Remove all but about 4 tablespoons of oil in the pan and fry the ground ingredients until fragrant.

Once fragrant and simmering, add in the coconut milk, water, 'tamarind' slices, lemongrass, and turmeric leaves, slowly bringing it to a boil. Add in the fried ground coconut and cook for another 2 minutes untill completely mixed.

Pour this mixture onto the fried fish and garnish with coriander leaves and serve.

FISH BAKED IN CORN SAUCE

1 kg (2.2 lbs) cod, garoupa or
   snapper fillet

Sauce
30 g (1 oz) butter
1 large white onion, chopped
   finely
4 cloves garlic, crushed
1½ teaspoons coriander powder
1½ teaspoons cumin powder
1½ teaspoons turmeric powder
1 teaspoon chilli powder
½ teaspoon black pepper
1 can creamed corn,
   approximately 425 g (15 oz)
1 tablespoon lemon juice
1 sprig coriander leaves, chopped

To make the sauce, melt the butter in a saucepan. Put in the onion and garlic and cook until soft. Stir in the other sauce ingredients

Preheat the oven to 180 °C (365°F) for about 10 minutes. Place the fish in a single layer in an oven-proof dish. Spoon the sauce over, reduce the oven heat to 150 °C (302°F) and bake the fish for about 25 minutes or until done.

AJ's Note: Baking of fish fillets is unlike baking a whole fish. I use a lower heat because the fillets cook faster and I don't want them to dry out.

STEAMED FISH OTAK OTAK

440 g (1 lb) fish fillet, cut into
   16 cubes
6 kaffir lime leaves (daun limau
   perut)
2 eggs, beaten
½ teaspoon salt
½ teaspoon sugar
¾ cup thick coconut milk
8 betel leaves (daun kaduk)

Blended together
2 root-ends lemongrass (serai)
4 candlenuts (buah keras)
1 tablespoon raw rice grains,
   soaked in hot water
1 teaspoon roasted shrimp paste
   (belacan)
5 red chillies
2 bird's eye chillies (chilli padi)
½ teaspoon peppercorns
2½ cm (1 in) turmeric or
   1 teaspoon turmeric powder
2½ cm (1 in) galangal (lengkuas)

Mix the blended ingredients with the sliced kaffir lime leaves, beaten eggs, and salt and sugar. Now add in the fish and coconut milk. Mix nicely.

Line a steaming dish with the betel leaves (daun kaduk). Pour in the mixture and steam for 15-20 minutes till firm.

AJ's Notes: Seafood otak-otak is another favourite. Instead of the fish, use a combination of 220 g (8 oz) cod, 100 g (3.5 oz) prawns and 100 g (3.5 oz) squid.

   As the cooking times of prawns and squids vary, I would recommend pre-cooking them. Marinate the prawns and/or squids in ¼ teaspoon salt and ½ teaspoon curry powder. Heat up 2 tablespoons oil and lightly fry the squid and prawns for 4 minutes. Set aside and add in ingredients according to the method for fish and steam for 15-20 minutes till firm.

FRAGRANT BUTTER PRAWNS

8 large prawns
3 tablespoons olive oil
3 tablespoons butter
2 sprigs coriander leaves,
  chopped
4 petals torch ginger bud
  (bunga kantan), chopped
4 cloves garlic, chopped
6 bird's eye chillies (chilli padi),
  thinly sliced
2 tablespoons grated coconut

Marinade
2 tablespoons Chinese rice wine
½ teaspoon ground black pepper
1 teaspoon palm sugar (gula
  Melaka)
1 root-end lemongrass (serai),
  thinly sliced
Pinch of salt

Remove the sac from the prawn heads and veins on the backs, leaving shells on. Marinate the prawns for 45 minutes. (See page 12 for detailed method of cleaning prawns.)

Heat the olive oil and when it is hot, fry the prawns. Add the marinade, ensuring that all the thinly sliced lemongrass are also poured in. Remove the prawns and the marinade once the prawns are orange and cooked.

Now add butter to the pan, lower flame, and include the coriander leaves, torch ginger bud, garlic and chillies. Stir fry until fragrant, then return the prawns to the pan. Taste, and adjust seasoning if necessary. Put in the grated coconut, toss to ensure the prawns are coated and serve.

AJ's Notes: This same recipe can be prepared with squid or crabs

Crabs
2 swimmer crabs (flower crabs) or crucifix crab (*Charybdis Feriatus*), approximately ½ kg (1.1 lbs) each.

Squids
4 medium-sized squids, cleaned and sliced into rings.

STUFFED FRIED FISH WITH SPICY MANGO SAUCE (RIGHT)

6 scomber (kembung) or
  torpedo scad (cencaru)
Juice of 4 calamansi limes
2 tablespoons cornflour
Oil for shallow frying
1 ripe mango, skinned and finely
  cubed

Pounded together
10 bird's eye chillies (chili padi)
Rind of 2 calamansi limes
1 teaspoon palm sugar
  (gula Melaka)

Blended together
8 shallots
4 cloves garlic
2 red chillis
2½ cm (1 in) ginger
1 root-end lemongrass (serai)

Remove the gills, and gut the fish (or have your fishmonger do it). Pat the fish dry with a kitchen towel. Turn the fish belly up and squeeze the juice of the calamansi lime on the fish and rub in the juices starting from the gills, down the spine and into the belly.

Place the pounded ingredients in a bowl and mix in the mango. Keep aside this spicy mango sauce until ready to serve the fish.

Coat the fish with cornflour, then using a teaspoon fill the bellies with the blended ingredients. Shallow fry the fish two at a time until crispy on the outside. These fish have no scales, hence it is normal for the skin to rupture.

Once the fish is ready, place them on a serving dish and spoon over the spicy mango sauce and serve.

THAI LEMON SHRIMPS

12 large prawns
2 tablespoons oil
¼ cup coconut milk
½ cup coriander leaves

Marinade
¼ cup Thai chilli sauce
1 tablespoon Thai chilli paste
  (Nam Prik Pao)
2 tablespoons lemon juice
2 teaspoons palm sugar
  (gula Melaka)
4 kaffir lime leaves (daun limau
  perut)
3 cloves garlic, minced
1 tablespoon fish sauce
1 teaspoon pepper

Remove sac from the prawn heads and vein on the back, leaving shells on. (See page 12 for detailed method of cleaning prawns.) You may remove the heads if you prefer. Place the prawns in a mixing bowl with the marinade and allow to marinate for 30 minutes to 4 hours.

Heat 2 tablespoons of oil in a pan and when hot, drop in the prawns, and all the marinade juices. Stir and cook for 5 minutes. Now add the coconut milk, half of the chopped coriander leaves. Stir and simmer for 5 minutes.

Season to taste, remove to a serving dish and garnish with the remainder of the coriander leaves.

PRAWNS IN CREAMY SAUCE

8 large king prawns
3 tablespoons oil
2 tablespoons butter
2 cloves garlic, chopped
1 stalk curry leaves
6 bird's eye chillies (chilli padi),
    chopped
1 cup thick coconut milk
½ teaspoon turmeric powder
3 sprigs Thai basil, leaves only
Sugar and salt to taste

Marinade
2 teaspoons Shaoxing rice wine
¼ teaspoon salt
2 teaspoons cornflour
½ teaspoon ground back pepper
1 teaspoon sugar

Remove the sacs from the prawn heads and veins from the backs, leaving shells on. Marinate for 15 – 20 minutes. (See page 12 for detailed method of cleaning prawns.)

Heat oil and stir fry the prawns till they become orange. Remove the prawns and set aside.

Add butter to the remaining oil and stir till melted. Now add the garlic, curry leaves and bird's eye chillies. Stir fry for 2 minutes till the butter begins to froth.

Lower flame and slowly add in the coconut milk, turmeric powder and Thai basil leaves. Simmer over low heat for 3 minutes, then season with sugar and salt to taste. Return the prawns to the pan, mix well and cook until the gravy thickens.

PRAWNS IN GLUTINOUS RICE

2½ cups glutinous rice (pulut)
½ cup coconut milk
½ teaspoon salt
1 tablespoon sugar
Banana leaves
Oil

Filling
½ kg (1.1 lbs) prawns, shelled
    and chopped finely
1 tablespoon dried prawns,
    toasted
10 shallots
2 cloves garlic
1 tablespoon coriander powder
3 teaspoons chilli paste
Salt and pepper to taste
1 cup grated coconut, dry fried
    till golden brown (kresik)

Wash the glutinous rice and soak it in water for 4 – 6 hours. The longer you wait, the better the rice will taste. Drain the rice and set aside.

Measure 2½ cups of water and combine it with ½ a cup coconut milk in a rice cooker. Add in the salt and sugar and turn on the rice cooker. Cook the rice for 20 minutes. Allow it to stand for at least five minutes after that. Remove from the cooker and cool.

To make the filling, pound the dried prawns, shallots and garlic until fine, then add in the coriander powder and chilli paste. Heat 3 tablespoons of oil in a frying pan and fry the pounded dried prawn mixture until brown, thereafter add in the prawns and season with salt and pepper to taste. Include the fried grated coconut and continue to stir fry until golden.

To assemble, cut the banana leaves into 7½ x 14 cm (3 x 6 in) pieces, and steam or run them over fire to soften them.

Spread about 1½ tablespoons of steamed rice onto each leaf and flatten lightly.

Place about 2 teaspoons of filling in the middle of the rice. Roll up and secure the flaps on both ends with toothpicks. Place the rolls in a steamer and steam for 10 minutes.

DAD'S SOYABEAN CLAMS

Soak the clams in a large bowl for about an hour. Add 1 tablespoon of flour into the water and mix – the clams will spit-out all the sand they hold. I have used this method for 25 years and it works.

1 kg (2.2 lbs) clams (*siput lala* or *remis*)

2 tablespoons oil

1 tablespoon finely diced garlic

1 tablespoon dried prawns, soaked in water then chopped finely

½ teaspoon ginger, finely diced

4 tablespoons chilli paste

1 tablespoon salted soya bean (tau cheong)

5 bird's eye chillies (chilli padi), diced

1½ teaspoons palm sugar (gula Melaka)

Heat the oil in a pan and fry the garlic until it is slightly brown, and then add in the dried prawns and ginger and simmer for 2 minutes. Now add in the chilli paste, salted soya bean and bird's eye chillies. You should have a thick paste.

Now add in the clams, mixing them with the paste thoroughly. Place a lid on the pan and allow it to simmer for 6–8 minutes until the clams open.

It is natural that the clams will release some water. Turn up the heat and continue to stir, coating clams well. Finally, add in 1½ teaspoons palm sugar and stir in. Ready to serve.

WHITE WINE AND BUTTER CLAMS

Growing up, a walk on the beach would often lead to searching for clams along the surf line. Keeping them in a bucket of sea water for a period of time prior to cooking ensured the shells discarded the sand within them.

Today, people would purchase clams fresh from the market, and adding a tablespoon of flour into plain water prior to soaking the clams is essential to removing the sand in the clams.

1 kg (2.2 lbs) clams (*siput lala* or *remis*)
2 tablespoons butter
6 cloves garlic, chopped finely
3 bird's eye chillies (chilli padi), diced
3 stalks flat parsley, chopped
½ teaspoon ginger, finely diced
1 cup white wine (my preference is Vermentino)
1½ tablespoon coconut cream
½ tablespoon palm sugar
12 Thai basil leaves

Heat the butter in a pan and fry the garlic, bird's eye chilli, parsley and ginger until slightly brown. Then add in the clams, mixing them with the ingredients thoroughly. Place a lid on the pan and allow to simmer for 6-8 minutes until you notice the clams opening.

It is natural that the clams will release some water. I recommend pouring out at least half the water before adding the white wine, coconut cream and palm sugar.

Turn up the heat and continue to stir, coating the clams well for another 5 minutes. Finally, toss in the basil leaves.

AJ's Notes: I do not recommend using dead clams, that is, clams that are refrigerated, pre-packed or stored in ice. It only takes one dead clam to spoil your day, or your entire dish.

Clam species: Siput Lala (*Cryptomya elliptica*), Siput Remis (*Donax cuneatus*), Siput Kapah (*Tapes belcheri*), Siput Kupang (*Meretrix meretrix*), Siput Retak Seribu (*Paphia textile*) and Siput Changkul (*Glauconome virens*).

INDEX

AJ's father is from Penang, of British blood with a touch of Burmese; his mother is of German and Dutch heritage from Sri Lanka. Theirs is a family of excellent cooks that explored favours and created recipes, and valued time in the kitchen together. Thus, AJ started cooking when he was 5.

At age 14, AJ began working as a kitchen apprentice but strayed into the world of Systems Engineering. However, he continued to add to his culinary palatte as he travelled throughout Asia for work and play. In 1996, he reached an epiphany in the Spice Market of Kochi when he fully appreciated that the core flavours of all the food of his childhood and youth, indeed the spectrum of Southeast Asian and Sri Lankan cuisines, would be impossible without the herbs and spices traded from the 14th century. From then, he has adapted, explored and created numerous dishes, focusing on the subtle and complex tastes derived from the flavouring ingredients of the region.

He returned to the hospitality industry in 2001 as a member of the team that reopened the restored Raffles Hotel. In 2004, he struck out on his own opening Spice Tree, a little shop selling curry puffs, to a roaring reception. Two months later, his puffs were judged best in Singapore by KF Seetoh and Violet Oon in a blind tasting organinsed by *The Straits Times*.

His food is redolent, familar yet new and exciting, so much so that his mother readily said: "Son, we may have taught you how to cook, but your cooking has attained another higher level."

AJ is now the Wine Ambassador, Asia, for Marco Bacci, the owner of three premier wineries of the Tuscan Valley. AJ is married and has a set of twins.